A Buddhist Path to Transforming Systems, Not Just Minds

The Social Justice of Conscious Prosperity

Dzambling Cho Tab Khen

(Dr. Alfredo Sfeir-Younis)

THE ZAMBULING INSTITUTE FOR HUMAN TRANSFORMATION

First edition, 2026
Cover design, book design and layout:
María Pia Moure Cominetti
www.sucedediseno.com
This book was set in the following typefaces:

Cover: Canela
           Miller
           Acumin Variable Concept
Interior: Georgia
           Lobster
           Acumin Variable Concept

Planet Healing Press
San Francisco, USA
ISBN: 979-8-9922083-6-8
© 2026 Alfredo Sfeir-Younis All rights reserved.

This book supports environmentally responsible publishing practices and is printed on FSC®-certified paper from responsibly managed forests.

This book is printed using Print-on-Demand (POD) technology, which supports sustainability by reducing waste, minimizing overproduction, and lowering the carbon footprint associated with traditional publishing methods.

Dedication

To my beloved teacher and spiritual father, Lama Gangchen Tulku Rinpoche. He made me discover the seeds I was to plant within the public domain of human collective transformation. These seeds are being fertilized by his teachings and by the various 'Social Teachings' of Lord Buddha. He showed me the Bodhisattva path to enlightenment.

To that invisible person who searches constantly for a body of wisdom vital to address humanity's challenges in this new millennium.

To those Buddhist monks who are in various corners of the planet, ready to redirect their inner attention and personal consciousness towards the power and wisdom of the primordial 'Social Teachings' of the Buddha.

To the inner voice that guides me while I am writing.

Always thank you.

With infinite gratitude to life in all its expressions.

Dzambling Cho Tab Khen

Note from the author

The future of humanity rests on the spiritual path we decide to walk for truth, justice, human self-realization, and collective transformation. To continue relying only on material economics, business, and politics for our happiness and inner well-being is a form of barbarism. This nonsense must stop. We are spiritual beings having a material experience.

Today, the world crisis is so profound that a major overhaul is needed.

A new planetary society is emerging. This society is characterized by a high level of porosity, where boundaries blur and where the interdependence among human beings, sentient beings, and nature is in its full expression. This new planetary society demands a heightened sense of humanity as a collective, which is not necessarily the arithmetic summation of individuals. This collective society is bound by shared energies, memories, behaviors, and consciousness.

> **The citizens of the world must awaken and participate directly in the transformations that are called for.**

Throughout my career in public policy, nationally and globally, I dedicated myself to crafting what, at the time, seemed to be the most effective collection of incentives, policies, investments, and institutional reforms to attain a unique form of sustainable society. In this process, I have realized that past approaches and instruments are no longer relevant.

As I deepened my understanding of policy-making, it became clear that underneath most individual and collective decisions, there was always a very specific "Social Doctrine" shaping that process.

Today, I am convinced that to prevent an extended human crisis of major proportions, or a global institutional collapse, we must bring about a new 'Social Doctrine'. I argue that "The Social Teachings" of Lord Buddha will bring humanity to its next level of collective consciousness. Those teachings are central in addressing the challenges of our times.

This book explores a sample of social teachings, as these are infinite in number. Teachings shared over 2,500 years ago. I believe they are even more pertinent today. The Buddha offered a wealth of human, social, economic, political, and institutional insights that remain deeply relevant.

As a Buddhist and as an economist by profession, this book represents my tiny contribution to a new world vision of what I see responding to a growing level of essential "collective awareness". A vision accompanied by a set of instruments and policies, vital to establish a "Buddhist Social Doctrine" for the new millennium.

This book is intended for Buddhists and non-Buddhists and for any person who feels deeply the profound urge for a renewed social doctrine on a planetary scale.

This book calls for a collective engagement in new forms of discernment, mindfulness, equanimity, and wisdom—i.e., all essential qualities to consolidating the full transition into our planetary society.

The moment is now. Tomorrow will be too late.

Dzambling Cho Tab Khen

Preface

"Buddhism is the missing mesh in our western evolution."

Levi-Strauss[1]

In the construct of our daily life, there is always a Social Doctrine which supports, guides, and nurtures our human collective activities like economics, politics, social, business, work, leisure, and institutional transformation and development. In the last few decades, we have witnessed all over the world the dominant power and role played by a "materialistic" and "individualistic" social doctrine[2]. Our contemporary body of social teachings, with their corresponding ethics and morals, in conjunction with the ideology they convey, has reached its limits of effectiveness in addressing the commonly shared collective issues humanity faces today. Based on promoting "individual materialism," this Social Doctrine contains the predicament that "more materiality is always better (material abundance)," and where "more" is also understood as a space of human success.

---

1   Antonio Minguez Reguera, "Una Aproximación al Budismo". Federación de Comunidades Budistas de España (FCBE).

2   In a very general sense, a 'social doctrine' is a formal or informal, implicit or explicit, proclamation framework, faith, ideology, or approach regarding what a given group, or a society as a whole, affirms about the nature and solutions of existing social issues. Here, it is said 'implicit' because many aspects of a social doctrine are not necessarily declared, but these do exist, and exercise a powerful influence in how we address the social issues within our societies. In some respects, one may also see a global social doctrine.

Globalization has accelerated this form of human and social development and transformation, with material wealth being concentrated in just a handful of people. Also, this materialistic doctrine has created some sort of illusion about the essence of "human progress" and "human wellbeing." It has been an illusion because it is all about "Having More" and not "Being More". Because we are in the path of 'Having' and not in the path of Being, most material wealth is created and obtained within a huge ethical and moral vacuum. Material growth and development must stop creating individual and social suffering, and establish the space for humanity's inner evolution.

Nobody can deny the importance of materiality, simply because our human life, in a human body, is anchored into various material realities and needs which are to be addressed and satisfied; e.g., food, shelter, clothing, and transport.

> **"The 200% Society":
> a society that is both
> materially and
> spiritually rich.**

Furthermore, as a result of today's social doctrine, we witness how people live in chaos, fueled by greed, suffering, diseases, depression, conflicts, violence, loss of identity, no sense of belonging, frustration, excessive accumulation, delusion, ecological destruction, even in the most materially rich nations of the world.

As a collective humanity, our greatest challenge is to establish what we may call "The 200% Society": a society that is both materially and spiritually rich. Reality demonstrates that the acquisition of "more matter" is not sufficient to establish a happy and contented society. In its teachings and principles, there is something fundamentally missing in today's Social Doctrine, implicitly or explicitly, which would ensure everlasting peace and happiness to all beings. Thus, there is a growing consensus that having more does not end up in being more.

At this very moment, we experience the human collective nature of a Planetary Society; e.g., what happens in one corner of the planet affects the entire planet. We live in a world with no boundaries. We live in a marked human collective.

This book is a wake-up call to Buddhist and non-Buddhist communities, and to all the people of goodwill, who are prepared to bring a new path to humanity. The Path of Being and Becoming. We must all make the effort to select and design strong and efficient strategic instruments to lay the foundation stone needed to construct a generation of human beings who become a beautiful temple of knowledge and wisdom in this 21st Century.

This must include the Buddha's teachings in economics, politics, business, human rights, social engagement, institutions, ecology, governance, sustainability... This book is the fruit of several decades of meditation, study, professional experience, and dedication to the type of human and social issues addressed here. To be faithful to a proper and accurate presentation, research and analysis are supported by a genuine effort to share the Buddha's teachings exactly as they were presented in the Suttas, the Vinaya, and other important Buddhist texts (e.g., The Dhammapada).

It important that the Buddhist communities find effective institutional mechanisms through which the Social Teachings of the Buddha are validated in one form or another. There must be some sort of global consensus[3].

> **It is essential that we understand much better the spiritual path of persons who want to help others (the human collective) to reach their enlightenment.**

Many canonical aspects of Buddhism — e.g., including validating the veracity of the teachings themselves — have been historically dealt with, institutionally, within the realm of six international gatherings, known as Buddhist Councils. Thus, to make sure that a new Buddhist Social Doctrine arises from a global consensus and validation, this book proposes the eventual consideration of a Seventh Buddhist

---

3   Again, an important component of the proposed social doctrine.

Council[4]. This Council must be conceived, called for, organized, and implemented soon. The aim of the Seventh Buddhist Council must be the consolidation of a universally agreed-upon Buddhist Social Doctrine. Perhaps, a step just before this Council ought to be a World Conference on the Social Teachings of the Buddha.

The original Social Teachings of the Buddha have proven to be transformative, both professionally and spiritually. The write-up process has surged from dialogues, reflections, and deep meditations to understand, practice, and self-realize the key messages presented here. Thus, the urgent understanding that we must make an effective effort and contribution to protect creation, and to prevent the destruction of sentient beings and nature. This realization must be all-encompassing, and not just focusing on human beings. We must take account of all manifestations of life, including the karmic and enlightenment paths of sentient beings, nature, beings of light, deities, gods, etc., no matter the reality or the level of consciousness they are in.

Today, it is essential that we understand much better the spiritual path of persons who want to help others (the human collective) to reach their enlightenment (this is often known as the Bodhisattva Path). It is that person who ends up being enlightened as he or she contributes to the process of enlightening others — i.e., the ultimate act of love, compassion, and generosity. The text emphasizes that we must contribute positively to all mutually interdependent relationship (the power of Being). The term mutuality refers mainly to the fact that any relationship cannot be just one-sided, as all of those involved in the relationship must become better off.

Humanity is at the vortex of a new form of spiritual transformation process and, thus, we are called to move, in full awareness and wisdom, into the inner self-realization of all forms of interdependence: the interdependence with our divine self (INTRA-BEING), with our col-

---

4   This is a fundamental proposal. Any Buddhist Social Doctrine must be validated, the same way other canonical aspects of Buddhism have been validated. The Seventh Buddhist Council will be that instance. A full chapter of this book is devoted to the content and scope of the council.

lective self (INTER-BING), and with all existing expressions of the individual (BEING) and collective Dharma (truth, wisdom, mission, ethics).

Humanity needs to attain a level of collective consciousness that enables every being to finally realize that everyone and everything are interdependent. The self-realization of this interdependent reality may allow us to know, strengthen, and expand our *"individual consciousness"*, *"collective consciousness,"* and *"nature's consciousness.*[5]*"*

> **It is not just a responsibility; it is also an ethical and moral obligation.**

These three expressions of consciousness form a fundamental "Triangle of Consciousness" for world healing, transcendental transformation, and change. In the end, we will realize that we are all One, and that this spiritual path contains the ultimate experience of Oneness; i.e., this is when our consciousness vibrates with the total unity of All.

One of the first realizations we may experience on this new path is that it is not just about the effective and spiritual practice of, for example, meditation, yoga, contemplation, mantras, chants...even though these practices contribute to the development and transformation of our inner spiritual mandala. These spiritual instruments will effectively transform our material world when we embrace all the dimensions of Dharma (the teachings). This is why we call Meditation immersed in Dharma: **"Meditation-Plus"**[6], i.e., a transformational instrument which will bring world peace and prosperity in all dimensions. As one great spiritual Guru once said to me: *"Even if you practice my form of yoga to perfection (e.g., positions, chants, mantras, mudras), you might never become a realized yogi."*

---

5   This surges from a higher level of consciousness that enables us to self-realize that nature is a living being and not a thing, with energy, behavior, memory, and consciousness.

6   This is a fundamental point, as many people, and even spiritual leaders, think that spirituality ends with the practice of spiritual instruments, born of a particular truth or Dharma. This is an incomplete picture; i.e., we must add to the instruments the whole Dharma!

It is worth repeating that the path to the self-realization of interdependence, indispensable to heal and transform the world, must consider the existence and contributions of "all manifestations of life" on this planet. We are one infinite space of collective consciousness. This is why human beings will never be healthy if nature is ill. The opposite situation is also true: Mother Nature will not be healthy if human beings are ill (physically, emotionally,...). It is in this sense this book advocates a new spirituality which is not anthropocentric. It cannot be, it should not be.

We must be aware of the need to bring The Social Teachings of the Buddha to this 21st Century, and demonstrate that they are as relevant now as they were then, at the time of the Buddha. These teachings are very rich in content and scope, and extremely applicable to our everyday activities.

It is not just a responsibility; it is also an ethical and moral obligation.

I bow to the Buddha
I devote this effort to the Buddha
I give unconditional love to the Buddha
I craft this entire book to the Buddha

Dzambling Cho Tab Khen

(Alfredo Sfeir-Younis)

Content

***Part* 3** **A PERSONAL LETTER TO YOU**

***Part* 4** **A BUDDHIST SOCIAL DOCTRINE: THE IMPERATIVE OF EDUCATION AND TRAINING**

Part

1

Immediate Priorities and Commitments

Chapter 1:

STRATEGIC CONCERNS

**"We must learn
to live together as brothers
or perish together as fools."**

Martin Luther King

THE GAP

Despite of all the material wealth and development we possess today, in Eastern and Western civilizations alike, we are witnessing a tremendous human and social decay. Throughout history, collective material progress has always been supported, explicitly or implicitly, by a powerful and unique Social Doctrine (e.g., rules of the game, alternative forms of engagement, various incentives, formal and informal teachings, ethics and morality, individual and collective values).

It is this Social Doctrine that supports and justifies the choices we make—public or private, individual or collective, spiritual or material-- to establish the different forms and mechanisms of wealth creation, accumulation, concentration, and equity, as well as the social values and ethics that accompany those choices. Judging by the results, this civilization is failing us today and, as a result, a huge gap has surfaced that must be filled soon.

Within this context, some key strategic questions are worth posing: Whose Social Doctrine (whose Spiritual Foundation) will fill the gap? What will the content of such a doctrine be?

In addressing these strategic questions, it seems rather clear that no existing political ideology should fill this gap. Today, people are demanding very different and meaningful answers.

The fundamental thesis of this book is that A Buddhist Social Doctrine, based on The Social Teachings of the Buddha, should have a great role to play in filling this present gap. As it will be demonstrated here, the Buddha offered profound insights and solutions to the various issues facing humanity today. This must become the century of Buddhism.

Also, the content and approach used to fill this gap will determine the future of Buddhism and the horizon of many Buddhist communities and monastic societies. If Buddhism fails to address the pressing questions and challenges confronting humanity today, its future relevance may be in jeopardy.

It is all about the Social Teachings in such areas as:
. **Economics** (wealth and welfare),
. **Politics** (political leadership),
. **Institutions** (community organizations),
. **Social** (policies and programs),
. **Business** (corporate management and leadership),
. **Governance** (self-governance, public and collective governance),
. **Human and Nature Rights**,
. **Sustainable Development**,
. **Ecology and Environment.**

Sometimes, the image projected by Buddhists and Buddhism around the world is one of being a group of people who abandoned or want to abandon the material world—i.e., that Buddhists are somehow in conflict with materiality.

However, the Buddha never promoted abandoning this material world. He never abandoned the material world himself. He stayed fully engaged and committed for several decades after his enlightenment. He stated that there is a big difference between abandoning the material world and abstaining from the negative aspects of this material world, like killing, stealing, lying, intoxicating oneself, sexual misconduct, etc. And, many Buddhas will come to this planet in the future.

Because of the unique foundations of a Buddhist Social Doctrine, this is expected to benefit not only human beings but also sentient beings and nature.

> **The Buddha never promoted abandoning this material world.**

THE WORLD

Today, we live in a very marked collective reality. For the first time in human history, we live in a Planetary Society. What happens in one corner of the planet affects all the rest, both over space and time. A world without frontiers[7].

However, we do not have a "Planetary Being" yet: someone who has become the other without losing their own identity. The human mind continues to think, express, and behave as if we human beings were separate entities (islands). In particular, we live in a world dominated by individual separateness. We are dominated by a powerful duality between the individual and the collective.

Many of us know by now that our human reality is characterized by "interdependence" and "interconnectedness". Today, both of these are in their maximum expressions. As a result, in our daily activities, it seems that the external effects of what we do are more prominent than the simple, direct, and immediate effects of a given human activity. For example, we drive cars and we generate tremendous pollution, health problems, congestion, and mental health issues. Thus, the net benefits to society of driving cars might be negative on certain occasions.

---

7   Until I became a young adult, to me, the predominant social doctrine was the catholic one. With the emergence of globalization and other institutional reasons, that doctrine began disappearing, to the point that nobody makes reference to it in private and public policy-making. For those who would like a brief summary of the thematic content of such a doctrine, please read: "Principles of Catholic Social Teachings". Micah Institute for Business and Economics. Seton Hall University (not dated). Attention is paid to: Consistent Ethic of Life; The Right to Life and Dignity of the Human Person; Call to Family, Community and Participation; Rights and Responsibilities; Option for the Poor and Vulnerable Dignity of Work and the Rights of Workers; Solidarity; Global Solidarity; Caring for God's Creation; and Toward a More Just Public Policy.

From another angle, the collective nature of our existence heightens the real importance that "Global Public Goods" play in our daily lives. Those are the goods and services which belong to, or affect, all of us, as a collective society of human beings, sentient beings, and nature. Examples of these Global Public Goods are: climate, global warming, biodiversity, glaciers, oceans, rivers, mountains, migration, natural forests, human security, peace, stability, etc. Thus, our individual and local realities do not constitute an island or a collection of separate, isolated entities.

Thus, notwithstanding the importance and benefits of our individual transformation and change, one cannot disregard what is happening at the collective level.

Within this collective reality, and as a foundation of such reality, there is an endowment of karmic accumulations (i.e., the fruits and impacts of our actions, be they past or present), which may come from this generation or past generations. These endowments are the result of positive and negative, internal and external, material and spiritual effects of our actions, habits, behavior, efforts, intentions, and the like. As we become part of the collective, we immediately realize that this collective is not empty. The collective not only has to address what our generation is doing, but also what all previous generations have done in the past.

Furthermore, the collective is more than the arithmetic summation or subtraction of the transformational effects of today's living beings.

"One plus one may be more, or less, than two." It may be geometric, or it may take any other form of accumulation. Therefore, the quality of our collective life may also depend on the nature, level, quality, and governance of our existing Collective Karmic Endowment[8].

---

8   The concept of "Karmic Endowment" is of fundamental importance, because it tells us that the collective is not an empty set. It is full of energy, memory, behavior, and consciousness, which affect us in many different ways. It has its own dynamic and personality. Social sciences focus on the nature of our collective all the time. Every individual reality has a corresponding collective reality at the same time. These are inseparable.

This is why, within the collective nature of our existence, we should stop and reflect for a moment.

To begin with, to live a collective reality presupposes the definition of various rights and shared responsibilities. They surge from the simple fact that the "nature of our mind", the "state of our mind", and the "levels of consciousness and awareness (SATI)" among all beings are not the same.

All of us have karmic debts and karmic accumulations of different natures and significance.

The Buddha expresses this reality through the teachings of ethics, the inner powers of abstentions (what to avoid doing), the practice of the self-realization of virtues, the practice of different forms of meditation, and the adoption and application of various material and spiritual skillful means available.[9]

> **To live a collective reality presupposes the definition of various rights and shared responsibilities**

Here, we focus on "social teachings" as these are always addressing the self and the other! Also known as the process of "INTER-BEING," human collective transformation[10].

The impacts on others, and not just the impacts on oneself. Also, Lord Buddha gave us advice and shared solutions which are to benefit all beings at the same time[11].

9　　Perhaps, this is one of the most important positive features of this book in relation to other attempts to distill some of the Buddha's social teachings. My professional experience has been a very important contributing factor.

10　　An excellent example of books that address a sample of social teachings of the Buddha is "The Buddha's Teachings on Social and Communal Harmony: An Anthology of Discourses from the Pali Canon (The Teachings of the Buddha. Amazon. December 13, 2016.

11　　Spirituality may begin within ourselves, but it is certainly not about us only. "The other" is an essential and inseparable lighthouse of our spiritual path.

The real interdependence manifests as if we were always crossing the borders between our human or non-human mandala (understood as the geometric expression of our inner and outer ecology). One case in point is that when a given person curses or insults another person, i.e., crossing the inner border and the emotional border of another being. Another case in point is a situation characterized by war and conflict, where one country (one collective) crosses the border of another country — a conflict between two mandalas. Yet, another case in point is that of a factory's source-pollution crossing all our borders; i.e., the factory produces a given product in one specific physical place and, out of its production, its embodied pollution (e.g., sulfur, CO_2, water pollution) ends up affecting people and sentient beings elsewhere[12].

> **To avoid living on the extremes, or living in duality, was a fundamental message of Buddha's teachings**

All the above demands changes in our behavior, habits, attitudes, policies, and incentives, so that the existing forms of interdependence among different actors end up bringing about the maximum possible material and spiritual welfare.

To avoid living on the extremes, or living in duality, was a fundamental message of Buddha's teachings. Positioning oneself on any extreme is a source of suffering.

Thus, we have learned that the collective nature of our existence demands a very elaborate new meaning, understanding, and interpretation of "The Middle Way", a central concept in Buddhism, whose essence was taught in the first discourse of the Buddha. As we better understand the dynamics of our collective existence, it is equally relevant to pay at-

---

12   This is a more complex issue than it may seem on the surface. Most economic indicators of human welfare, like Gross National Product, are measured by the immediate and direct impact of any economic activity. The second and third round effects of those activities are never accounted for by those indicators of human welfare. Today, the magnitude of those negative external effects is far superior to the direct impacts in the first place.

The Law of
KARMA

The Law of
INTERDEPENDENCE

The Law of
CORRESPONDENCE

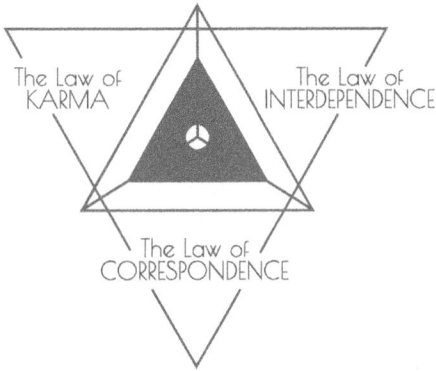

tention to all the possible dimensions of "The Noble 8-Fold Path": collective vision, collective intent, collective language, collective action, collective behavior, collective effort, collective mindfulness, and collective meditation.

Thus, as we dig into this collective reality, we will find at least two components: the thread which comes directly from individual behaviors and actions (creates collective reality), and the thread which comes from the collective endowments (creates individual reality), behaviors, and actions of a totality. Both have their relative impacts within our human reality.

This is why many of us state it is very relevant to focus on the refinement of the mind and the transcending of consciousness, which comes from the recognition and experience of The Social Dimensions of Suffering (i.e., social dukkha). This is because our "outer ecology" is intimately connected with our "inner ecology", something that is relevant to all beings.

This is often known as The Law of Correspondence, which states that "the inner is like the outer and the outer is like the inner."

The bridge from the individual to the collective is essentially defined by:
- **The Law of Interdependence (LOI)**
- **The Law of Correspondence (LOC)**
- **The Law of Karma (LOK)**

To summarize, the greatest challenge of Buddhism is to move rapidly forward with instruments and practices to advance the individual power of transformation and, simultaneously, and with a Buddhist global sense and response to humanity's problems (collective transformation).

Thus, within a policy context, it is not only relevant to self-realize compassion at the individual level, but also, and simultaneously, to commit oneself to the creation of a Compassionate Society.

At a more refined level, the Buddha expresses the same principle: the creation of material wealth must be simultaneously accompanied by an Ethic of Wealth creation. This is the same Social Ethics that should support any notion of human rights.

In a figurative sense, this challenge of addressing the individual and the collective at the same time could be illustrated by a scenario where one throws a big stone into a still lake. In that scenario, there are two impacts of the stone on the still lake: one, the stone going to the bottom of the lake, transcending all possible limitations; and the other, the 'splash effect' of the stone, whereby millions of ripples go everywhere on the surface of that still lake. Both of these impacts act simultaneously. They exist together: the transformation at the individual level and the transformation at the collective level.

To address those abovementioned challenges is not only our obligation as Buddhists, but also it is the essential legacy we are to leave for this and future generations.

TO REMEMBER

This is the great century of Buddhism, particularly within the public domain. Its unique content, scope, and skillful means, coupled with the downfall of many other spiritual and social doctrines, put the Buddha's social teachings at the forefront of policy-making and strategy design, and implementation. It is, perhaps, the only century for Buddhism as far as public and private policy at the local, national, regional, and global levels are concerned. If we do not do something now, it will be too late.

My spiritual teachers pushed me into creating new narratives and establishing an innovative social grammar. In all cases, to change the world by bringing spirituality into economics, politics, and society, with special emphasis on Buddhist spirituality. I have been dedicating nearly half a century of my life to these very crucial thematic areas. Through understanding, practicing, and self-realizing, my spiritual path has been enriched and greatly expanded to gradually approach another state of higher consciousness.

Thus, the proposal made here represents something other than uncharted territory. The absence of this Buddhist Social Doctrine (BSD) within the practices of daily human activities (as listed before), is due mainly to: a lack of knowledge by decision and policy-makers alike; a misunderstanding of the boundaries of Buddha's teachings; or simply, and a disregard for what the Buddha taught about the attributes and problems of our daily social livelihood, collective behavior, and societal efforts. Today, there is a misguided impression that the Buddha only taught about the personal inner unfoldment, and about how to expand individually-tailored human consciousness attainments.

There is this idea that everything in Buddhism is only about individual enlightenment, and not about collective enlightenment, surging from a set of practices, initiations, realizations, power of silence, inner healing, change in habits, abstentions, merits... There is no doubt that the beginning of the spiritual path must commence with a solid and sustainable foundation of one's individual path towards enlightenment. However, this exclusive emphasis has led to focusing quasi-exclusively on the individual aspects of Buddhism.

A case in point is reflected by what many believe are the causes and conditions of (individual) suffering. In today's world, experience shows that most causes and conditions of suffering are social and collective in nature (something also expressed above). Social suffering is one key ingredient of the 21st century's societies. Examples of this social suffering abound; e.g., just think about COVID-19, climate change, biodiversity depletion, instability and insecurity, social and ecological migration, exclusion and marginalization, violation of human and nature

> **Today, there is a misguided impression that the Buddha only taught about the personal inner unfoldment**

rights, war and conflicts, inadequate health policies and services, lack of education, poor water and sewerage systems, moral and ethical vacuums, etc.

Today, it is almost impossible to separate individual suffering from collective suffering! Simply stated, there are no boundaries any longer. This absence of boundaries is more evident than ever before when one tries to define and assign key responsibilities for what is happening in the world today. Individually shared responsibilities must be able to collectively address the Social Factors of Suffering as an essential spiritual attribute and as an ingredient to be considered, both in a material and spiritual sense.

The claims made here have neither surged as outcomes of purely personal interpretations regarding the nature of Buddhism as a spiritual path, nor as a set of personal re-interpretations of Buddha's teachings. The position here on a social doctrine is not an interpretative one. As a matter of consideration, what is presented and concluded here comes directly from the Buddha's teachings, as expressed by a large number of sutras. Perhaps, this is the single most important contribution of the discussions and conclusions presented and advocated here.

> **It is almost impossible to separate individual suffering from collective suffering!**

THE SPIRITUAL MISSION

To make Buddha's social teachings universally accessible on all continents; to create the networking conditions necessary to inner-empower policymakers through new forms of collective spiritual wisdom, to create a harmonious planetary livelihood; and to alleviate human individual and social suffering through the enhanced power of collective consciousness. It is a commitment to create a "Global Vinaya" (mandate, rules of engagement, ethics and morals, right action and behavior). At the time of the Buddha, he was committed to a Vinaya as a central pillar in the formation of monastic societies.

THE VISION CALLED FOR

To move from the paradigm of "Individual Materialism" to inner-conscious societies governed not by one, but by three interdependent and inseparable bodies of laws: human, natural, and spiritual. Through Buddhist social wisdom and practices, as taught directly by the Buddha, and still very relevant for the challenges we face in this 21st Century, the ideas proposed here will spiritually reconnect private and public, inner and outer, material and non-material, individual and collective economics, politics, business, and institutions.

The book offers a path committed to the construction and emergence of a new collective reality, based on a different set of collective values and principles, so that human beings, sentient beings, and nature attain their full potential. From all of these, new narratives will emerge, which will deeply change the process of transformation of all manifested forms of life.

OUR COMMITMENT

We are inseparable, interdependent selves. Our true and transcending nature unfolds when every being unfolds. The unfolding process has human, natural, and spiritual attributes in all their possible expressions of life. Then, the road to the solutions of our shared problems also rests on our collective consciousness and collective actions and deeds. Thus, the nature of a powerful Buddhist Social Doctrine captures this inseparable interdependent reality among all expressions of life, and all manifested and non-manifested forms of consciousness. The consciousness of human beings, sentient beings, and nature, all inseparable as ONE.

If one is to make a policy statement, Buddhist spirituality is not oriented solely to the self-realization, for example, of compassion (KARUNA), but simultaneously, with a commitment to construct a compassionate society. In essence, we all must experience both the individual and the collective forms of enlightenment at the same time. We all must practice "The Spirituality of the Other." We all must establish the grounds for the self-realization of mutuality, so that every being is better off and no one is worse off.

There is no separation between spirituality and economics, politics, business, or institutions. The practice of politics or economics without spirituality (e.g., a practice within an ethical and moral vacuum) becomes a suicidal path for humanity, and any spiritual practice outside the domain of daily life—economic or political contexts—becomes just another theoretical and abstract proposition.

> **There is no separation between spirituality and economics, politics, business, or institutions.**

Buddhist teachings invite us to take responsibility not only for ourselves, but also for the entire community and ecosystem. That is the essence of KARUNA. Then, we must work together for social rights and justice, and seek that our spiritual practice becomes part and parcel of social change.

THE VALUES

Any dimension of a given spiritual path and social doctrine is always supported by a collection of values, be they individual or collective, material or spiritual. The ideas proposed here are greatly influenced by the values of generosity, cooperation, interdependence, mutuality, love, compassion, justice, rights, trust, equanimity, rigor, and more. As such, those values are not a "thing" but "a state of being" and must be self-realized. The proposals made here are expected to accelerate the processes of self-realization of those values.

Chapter 2:

CALLING FOR A 'SEVENTH BUDDHIST COUNCIL'

"Do not dwell in the past,
do not dream of the future,
concentrate the mind
on the present moment."

"The trouble is,
you think you have time."

"If you light a lamp for somebody,
it will also brighten your path."

Lord Buddha

This is a call to all Buddhists and scholars around the world to bring about a Seventh Buddhist Council (SBC) to identify, establish, and validate the most important "Social Teachings of the Buddha".

As part of their institutional paths, governance instruments, and formal dialogues, most worldwide spiritual movements and world religions consider 'calls for council meetings'. This is a traditional institutional mechanism, and in Buddhism, this is not an exception.

This chapter presents the essential ingredients and main contributions of the six Buddhist Councils that took place during the last 2600 years, since the passing away of the Buddha. Thus, it summarizes the main goals and attainments of those previous six councils. After doing so, this chapter justifies the call for a Seventh Council, which ought to be fully devoted to the Social Teachings of the Buddha, and details the content and scope of such a council. It charts a road towards its implementation.

BACKGROUND

Buddhist councils are historic instances where monks and other Buddhist scholars recognize and legitimize the teachings of the Buddha, incorporate different rules of behavior within monastic communities, and promote unity among these different communities (the Sangha). All with the view to preserve, contribute, and disseminate knowledge, wisdom, scriptures, practices, and behavior, and to develop Buddhism. These councils have also been an instrument and a vehicle to settle innumerable disputes and validate alternative interpretations around the Buddha's teachings.

As such, these councils have played a crucial role in the lineage's transmission of the teachings and in the development of different Buddhist traditions.

The First Council happened very soon after the passing away of the Buddha, in ancient India. Something truly unique and fundamental. Till today, there have been six councils implemented (some talk about a larger number of councils and others less). It is clear that the councils have been instrumental in shaping the real history and evolution of Buddhism, upholding the purity and authenticity of the teachings. In most cases, the councils have served as a precious moment of profound reflection, discussion of various issues and concerns, and as instances for consensus-building on matters of doctrine, ethics, and practice.

As a historic fact, after the Buddha passed away (i.e., *the Mahaparinibbāna*), his chief disciple *Mahākassapa* was on his way to Kushinagar, with approximately 500 disciples. It took him a week to get to where the Buddha's physical body was. On the way, he happened to experience the foolishness of some members of the *Sangha*.

This was the case of a monk named Subhadda, who became very happy that the Buddha died so that no exigencies or individual and communal responsibilities were to be strictly obeyed any longer. Because of that event, *Mahākassapa* became concerned with the possible twisting of the Buddha's teachings and with the potential misrepresentation of the Buddha's codes of ethics and morals. The situation was per-

> It is clear that the councils have been instrumental in shaping the real history and evolution of Buddhism

ceived as a real cause for a possible Dhamma's downfall. This is why *Mahākassapa* concluded that it was urgent that all the statements of the Buddha be gathered and compiled together.

At that time, it was well known that the presence of rebellious monks during the lifetime of Buddha. Buddhist texts also show the attempts to kill the Buddha by *Devadatta* and the problems that surged from the behavior of Channa, who refused teachings and other instructions (remember he was the charioteer of the Buddha — perhaps, his first teacher). There are other examples of these conflicting situations.

This is how the First Council *(Sangayana)* was born, only three months after the Buddha was cremated. The First Council took place at the Sattapanni Cave in Rajgir.

THE FIRST BUDDHIST COUNCIL

The First Buddhist Council (circa 483 BCE) was convened shortly after the Buddha's passing in Rajagaha, India, and conducted under the patronage of King Ajatasatu of the Haryanka Dynasty. The purpose of this council was to recite and codify the Buddha's teachings, known as the Dhamma (knowledge, truth, teachings) and the Vinaya (discipline, behavior, codes of ethics). As stated above, this council was presided over by *Mahākassapa* and attended by approximately 500 enlightened monks. The teachings were orally transmitted and organized into the Tripitaka (meaning "the three baskets"): Sutta Pitaka (discourses), Vinaya Pitaka (monastic rules), and Abhidhamma Pitaka (philosophical analysis). The recitation and preservation of the teachings were done orally, as writing was not yet widely practiced in ancient India.

Because of his remarkable memory, Ananda, the Buddha's cousin and personal attendant, played a key role in reciting the teachings. The council lasted for seven months, during which time the entire Buddhist canon was recited and verified by the assembled monks. If there were any discrepancies or disagreements in the teachings, these were resolved through discussion and consensus among those participating in the council.

The council also produced the first written version of the Buddhist scriptures, inscribed on palm leaves and stored for future generations.

The teachings regarding the Vinaya (rules and regulations for the monks) were well absorbed and understood by *Upāli* (another senior disciple). In the end, this contribution was accepted by all. It is relevant to add that there were charges made against Ananda as it was known that he could not have an adequate formulation of the so-called "minor precepts," among other things. The origin of these disputes has its roots in the last teaching of the Buddha, where he stated through Ananda that: "if the Sangha has a desire to abrogate the lesser and minor rules after his demise, that he permits."

The First Buddhist Council marked the beginning of the Buddhist monastic tradition and the formalization of the teachings

The First Buddhist Council, which lasted nearly seven months, has been considered a very important event in the history of Buddhism because it marked the beginning of the Buddhist monastic tradition and the formalization of the teachings. It is important to acknowledge that the Buddha never nominated a successor and that there was not a single person who embodied all the teachings of the Buddha.

As is well known, some historians doubt whether the texts we have today are the same as those recited in the First Buddhist Council. Even more, some doubt that this council took place. The source of its existence comes from one section of the Pali Vinaya called the Cullavagga. Also, some question the empowerment of Ananda, as he was not enlightened at the time of the Buddha's *Mahāparinirvāṇa*. The story goes that Ananda was enlightened through the night before the council.

THE SECOND BUDDHIST COUNCIL

The Second Buddhist Council (circa 383 BCE) was held at *Vaiśālī*, India, about a century after the First Council. The main aim of this council was to address disputes over several aspects of the existing monastic discipline (practices and rules). This council was presided over by *Śābakāmī*, and the main objective was to discuss ten disputed points under the Vinaya Pitaka.

The first major split happened here — two groups that would later evolve into *Theravāda* and *Mahāyāna*. The first group was called Thera (meaning Elder in Pali). They wanted to preserve the teachings of Buddha in the original spirit. The other group, called *Mahāsāṃghika* (Great Community), interpreted the Buddha's teachings more liberally. The council resulted in the formation of the *Sthāvirā* (Elders) and the *Mahāsāṃghika* (Great Assembly) schools, marking the real first split in the Buddhist community. The patronage was given by King *Kalāsoka* of the *Śiśunāga* Dynasty.

Furthermore, the Second Buddhist Council was convened to also address the so-called "TEN POINTS" dispute as regards some relaxed rules of discipline followed by certain monks, especially the monks living in the area of *Vaiśālī*. The ten points were related to storing salt in a horn, eating after midday, carrying official acts when the assembly was incomplete, using gold and silver, among others.

The schism at the Second Council had far-reaching consequences for the development of Buddhist schools and sects, leading to the formation of distinct lineages and doctrinal differences within the monastic community. The division between the *Sthāvirā* and *Mahāsāṃghika* schools set the stage for further schisms and diversification of Buddhist traditions in the centuries that followed.

THE THIRD BUDDHIST COUNCIL

The Third Buddhist Council (circa 250 BCE) was convened by Emperor Ashoka in *Pāṭaliputra*, India. Emperor Ashoka, a devout Buddhist ruler who sought to promote and protect the teachings of the Buddha, played a crucial role. This is a very important historical fact. The council was called to correct, clear, and purify the greater *Saṅgha* from what was seen as "corrupt practices" and "heresies" that had emerged since the Second Buddhist Council. It is said that one of the council's most relevant outcomes was the standardization of the *Tripiṭaka* and the sending of missionary monks to spread Buddhism to various regions, including Sri Lanka and Southeast Asia.

> **The main aim was to address disputes over several aspects of the existing monastic discipline**

The council was presided over by Moggalliputta Tissa, and attended by leading Buddhist monks from various regions, including representatives of different Buddhist schools and lineages. The Third Buddhist Council resulted in the compilation and recitation of the *Tripiṭaka*, which included the Sutta *Piṭaka* (discourses), Vinaya *Piṭaka* (monastic rules), and Abhidhamma *Piṭaka* (philosophical analysis). The council also established a formal system for the transmission and preservation of the Buddhist scriptures, ensuring the continuity and integrity of the teachings for future generations. The council's decisions and initiatives helped to consolidate the foundations of *Theravāda* Buddhism and establish a framework for the propagation of the Dhamma to different parts of the Indian subcontinent and beyond.

The final version of the *Tripiṭakas* was completed in this council: the last Abhidhamma *Piṭaka* (which dealt with the philosophy of the Buddha) was compiled during this council. The *Kathāvatthu* was composed by Moggalliputta Tissa, in which he set out to disprove the wrong opinions and theories of sects. King *Aśoka* sent Thera monks, knowledgeable in the Dhamma and Vinaya, to nine different countries for the spread of the Dhamma. The Dhamma missions of these monks succeeded and influenced civilizations and cultures.

THE FOURTH BUDDHIST COUNCIL

The Fourth Buddhist Council (1st century CE) was held in Kashmir, India, under the patronage of King *Kaniṣka*. This council was convened with the principal idea to address various doctrinal disputes and clarify some of the teachings of the Buddha. All deliberations were conducted in Sanskrit. The council resulted in the very important compilation of commentaries and sub-commentaries on the *Tripiṭaka*, as well as the establishment of the *Sarvāstivāda* and *Mahāsāṃghika* schools.

The Fourth Buddhist Council was attended by leading Buddhist monks, scholars, and practitioners from various regions, representing different Buddhist schools and traditions. The council was presided over by the venerable monk Vasumitra, who played a key role in organizing and overseeing the proceedings. As in previous councils, it aimed to compile commentaries and sub-commentaries on the *Tripiṭaka* to provide a systematic and comprehensive understanding of the Dhamma (teachings) and Vinaya (monastic discipline).

The Fourth Buddhist Council made significant contributions to the preservation and dissemination of the Buddha's teachings, as well as the development of Buddhist scholarship and philosophy. The council's emphasis on clarifying doctrinal ambiguities and promoting doctrinal unity laid the foundation for the continued transmission and propagation of Buddhism in different regions and cultural contexts. This council resulted in the division of Buddhism into two sects, namely, *Mahāyāna* (the Greater Vehicle) and *Hīnayāna* (the Lesser Vehicle).

> **The Tripitaka:**
> **The Sutta Pitaka**
> **(discourses)**
> **The Vinaya Pitaka**
> **(monastic rules)**
> **The Abhidamma Pitaka**
> **(philosophical analysis)**

THE FIFTH BUDDHIST COUNCIL

The Fifth Buddhist Council (1871 CE) was held in Mandalay, Burma (Myanmar), under the patronage of King Mindon. It was attended by 2,400 monks, presided over by three Elders — the Venerable *Mahāthera* Jagarabhivamsa, the Venerable Narindabhidhaja, and the Venerable *Mahāthera* Sumangalasami. The council was convened to recite and preserve the *Theravāda Tipiṭaka*, which had been brought to Burma from Sri Lanka. The council resulted in the meticulous transcription and preservation of the Pali Canon, as well as the compilation of commentaries and sub-commentaries. The council aimed to meticulously transcribe and preserve the Pali Canon in written form to ensure its accuracy and authenticity for future generations. The council lasted for five months.

The Fifth Buddhist Council was attended by prominent *Theravāda* monks, scholars, and practitioners from Burma and other *Theravāda* Buddhist countries. The council was presided over by a committee of senior monks, led by the chief prelate, *Aggamahāpaṇḍita*. Its objective was to recite all the teachings of the Buddha and examine whether any of them had been altered, distorted, or neglected. The entire recitation was captured in marble slabs, about 729 of them. All the slabs were housed in beautiful miniature *Piṭaka* pagodas. It is located on the grounds of King Mindon's Kuthodaw Pagoda at the foot of Mandalay Hill.

The Fifth Buddhist Council resulted in the meticulous transcription and preservation of the entire Pali Canon, including the commentaries and sub-commentaries on the scriptures. The council's efforts led to the publication of the *Tipiṭaka* in printed form, making the Buddhist scriptures more widely accessible to monks, scholars, and lay practitioners.

The council also contributed to the dissemination of the teachings of *Theravāda* Buddhism to a broader audience, both within Burma and in other *Theravāda* Buddhist countries. The council's meticulous transcription and publication of the Pali Canon have provided a valuable

> **Objective: to recite all the teachings of the Buddha**

resource for the study and practice of *Theravāda* Buddhism, serving as a foundation for the preservation of the Dhamma for future generations.

THE SIXTH BUDDHIST COUNCIL

The Sixth Buddhist Council (1954–1956 CE) was held in Yangon, Burma (Myanmar), under the patronage of Prime Minister U Nu. The council was convened to recite and revise the *Tipiṭaka* and its commentaries in order to preserve the teachings of *Theravāda* Buddhism. The council resulted in the publication of the entire Pali Canon and its commentaries in printed form, as well as the dissemination of Buddhist texts to a wider audience. The council commemorated 2,500 years of Buddhism. The entire text of the Pali *Theravāda* canon was recited and reviewed by the assembly of monks from different countries.

The Sixth Buddhist Council was called at Kaba Aye in Yangon (formerly Rangoon) in 1954, 83 years after the fifth one was held in Mandalay. Then, the Prime Minister, the Honourable U Nu, authorized the construction of the *Maha Paṭṭhāna Guha*, the "great cave," an artificial cave very much like India's Sattapanni Cave, where the first Buddhist Council had been held. Upon its completion, the Council met on 17 May 1954. This council was unique insofar as the monks who took part in it came from eight countries. The traditional recitation of the Buddhist Scriptures took two years, and the *Tripiṭaka* and its allied literature in all the scripts were painstakingly examined, their differences noted down, and the necessary corrections made, and all the versions were then collated.

The council's efforts led to the dissemination of the revised and standardized version of the Pali Canon to a wider audience, both within Burma and in other *Theravāda* Buddhist countries. The council also contributed to the promotion of scholarship and research in the field of *Theravāda* Buddhism, encouraging the study and practice of the Buddha's teachings. The council's revision and publication of the *Tripiṭaka* have provided a valuable resource for monks, scholars, and lay practitioners interested in studying and practicing *Theravāda* Buddhism. The council's efforts have contributed to the ongoing transmission and propagation of the Dhamma, serving as a foundation for the preservation of the Buddha's teachings for future generations.

THE ULTIMATE GOAL: A PLANETARY VINAYA

The previous Buddhist councils paid great attention to the conservation and purity of the teachings (personal and social teachings) as well as the rules and regulations of the monastic societies in question. This is to say, the proof of their existence, the content, and its application. These have been essential in defining the content and scope of Buddhism today.

The call for a Seventh Buddhist Council should open the space and purity to host all the Social Teachings of the Buddha, with the view to establishing progressively a Buddhist Social Doctrine, which will be made available to all humanity, Buddhists and non-Buddhists alike.

The Seventh Buddhist Council will have a fundamental canonical dimension in that the origin of this Social Doctrine must be traced directly to the teachings of the Buddha.

In addition, the Seventh Buddhist Council must construct a Planetary Vinaya capable of establishing a form of planetary livelihood that will benefit human beings, sentient beings, and nature. Because of the serious environmental constraints facing most countries in the world, one dimension of the concept of a Planetary Vinaya would, by necessity, refer to environmentally and socially sustainable livelihood (ways of life on this planet), following Buddhist principles like love, compassion, wisdom, joy, equanimity, non-violence, and respect for all forms of life.

The Planetary Vinaya would, in this respect, consider forms and characteristics like:

I. Respect for all expressions of life and, thus, living in harmony with nature and treating all living beings with compassion and respect.

II. Conscious production and consumption, and being aware that growing faster of exploiting more is not better, and that we must create health and happiness via productive activities and the elimination of suffering.

III. Sustainable food production and distribution activities and practices, embracing the use of agricultural methods that enhance land and water, and protect, conserve, and promote biodiversity.

IV. Use of renewable energy, particularly non-conventional renewable sources of energy, like hydrogen, solar, wind, or hydroelectric energy, instead of fossil fuels.

V. Waste reduction, reuse, and recycling for a circular economy.

VI. Sustainable transport in the public and private sectors, with special emphasis on electric public transport, cycling, walking, and reduced use of motor vehicles.

VII. Green infrastructure practices, with sustainable building materials and environmentally friendly construction techniques.

VIII. Water resource awareness, conservation, and management, given the water crisis facing most communities around the world.

IX. Establishment of alternative systems of environmental education and training, by changing the curricula from kindergarten to university level of education.

X. Support for the conservation, protection, management, and rights of nature, contributing to the preservation of natural ecosystems and the protection of biodiversity.

The Planetary Vinaya will embrace incentives, rules, regulations, rights, responsibilities, and guidelines that would govern planetary life. It would serve as a code of conduct that ensures discipline, harmony, and ethical behavior in all aspects of daily life. It will become an essential component of Buddhist and non-Buddhist practice, cultivating merits and virtues such as mindfulness, humility, and compassion. In recent years, there has been a growing interest in the idea of a Planetary Vinaya, which seeks to apply the principles of the Vinaya to address contemporary global challenges.

Thus, the concept of a Planetary Vinaya will extend the traditional understanding of the Vinaya beyond the boundaries of the monastic community, to encompass all living beings and the environment. It should emphasize the interconnectedness of all beings and the importance of ethical conduct (social ethics) in promoting harmony and sustainability. By applying the principles of a Buddhist type of Vinaya to address issues such as social justice, environmental degradation, and conflict resolution, it offers a holistic approach to creating a more just, compassionate, and sustainable world.

In a Planetary Vinaya, the principle of no harm *(ahiṃsā)*, which prohibits the intentional taking of life, will be extended to embrace the protection of all living beings and the environment. This will contribute to the well-being of the planet and create a more sustainable future.

Another important aspect of the Planetary Vinaya will be the practice of equanimity and generosity *(dāna)*, enabling us to address issues of social inequality and poverty. For instance, providing food, shelter, and healthcare to those in need can help alleviate suffering and promote human rights and social justice.

The Planetary Vinaya will emphasize the importance of ethical conduct and mindfulness in all activities. This will enable inner peace and collective wisdom everywhere. The Planetary Vinaya will help to navigate the complexities of life and respond skillfully to challenges such as conflict and injustice. By applying the principles of the traditional Vinaya in our daily lives, we will contribute to the welfare and enlightenment of all beings on the planet.

The concept of a Planetary Vinaya will offer a revolutionary approach to addressing the pressing challenges facing our world today. By applying the principles and social teachings of the Buddha, one would promote non-harming, generosity, ethical conduct, and mindfulness, so that we can create a more just, compassionate, and sustainable society.

Such a Vinaya will create full awareness of our complete and unavoidable interconnectedness with all beings and the importance of living in harmony with the natural world. By embodying these principles in our lives, we can contribute to the well-being of the planet and work towards a more peaceful and sustainable future.

OUR HUMAN COLLECTIVE REALITY

One key aspect of the Seventh Buddhist Council will be to recognize and self-realize that, today, we live in a very marked collective reality. For the first time in human history, we live in a planetary society. What happens in one corner of the planet affects all the rest. We do not have a planetary being yet: someone who can become the other without losing their own identity. Most people continue to behave as if they are separate islands, instead of understanding that our human reality is characterized by total "interdependence" and "interconnectedness" in their maximum expression.

Today, in our daily life, we witness how the external effects (i.e., positive or negative impacts on others) of what we do are more prominent than the direct, simple, and immediate effects of a given human activity (e.g., industrial pollution). Thus, the collective nature of our existence heightens the real importance of our **"Global Public Goods"**; i.e., those goods and services that belong to, or affect, all of us as a collective society of human beings, sentient beings, and nature. Examples of these are: climate, global warming, biodiversity, glaciers, oceans, rivers, mountains, migration, security, etc.

At this very moment, the planet is facing serious collective challenges. Notwithstanding the vital importance of individual transformation, we cannot disregard what is happening at the level of the collective. There is an "endowment of karmic accumulations," which comes from this generation and past generations. These karmic endowments result from positive and negative internal and external effects of our actions *(karma)*. Thus, the collective space is not void, and, therefore, we must address what our generation is doing as well as what is happening with the governance of our Collective Karmic Endowments. The Buddha expresses this reality through the teachings of ethics, abstentions, precepts, and many other skillful means. These are teachings which always address "the other"—the impacts on others! The Buddha brought teachings and practices that are to benefit all beings at the same time.

All the above demands change in our behavior, habits, attitudes, policies, and incentives, so that existing forms of interdependence end up bringing about the maximum possible material and spiritual welfare (i.e., to human beings, sentient beings, and nature). This is the reason why many Buddhists today advocate that it is also relevant to focus on the transformation and transcending which comes from recognizing The Social Dimensions of Suffering *(DUKKHA)*: the fact that our "outer ecology" is intimately connected with our "inner ecology."

Thus, we are inseparable interdependent selves, including all human beings, sentient beings, nature, and the spiritual attributes in all their possible expressions of life. Thus, solutions to humanity's problems also rest on our collective consciousness and collective actions and deeds.

The construction of a Buddhist Social Doctrine, through the Seventh Buddhist Council, is to capture this inseparable interdependent reality among all expressions of life, and among all manifested and non-manifested forms of consciousness.

Then, the greatest challenges of Buddhism are: (i) to rapidly move forward with those instruments and practices which enhance the individual power of transformation (meditation), and (ii) to simultaneously move forward by providing a Buddhist global response to humanity's problems. Thus, it is not only relevant to self-realize compassion at the individual level, but also, and simultaneously, to commit oneself to the creation of a Compassionate Society.

> **Our "outer ecology" is intimately connected with our "inner ecology"**

The Seventh Buddhist Council could be, in a figurative sense, the instance in which we face the challenge of addressing the individual and the collective at the same time.

This could be represented by the throwing of a big stone into a totally still lake. There is a double effect of the impact of such a stone on the still lake: (i) one from the stone going to the bottom of the lake, transcending all possible limitations, and (ii) another, the splash effect of the stone, whereby millions of ripples go everywhere on the surface of that still lake. Both of these impacts act simultaneously. They exist together: (i) the transformation at the individual level and (ii) the transformation at the collective level.

THIS IS THE CENTURY OF BUDDHISM

This is the century of Buddhism, particularly within the public domain. Its unique content, scope, and skillful means, coupled with the downfall of many other spiritual social doctrines, put the Buddha's teachings at the forefront of policy-making and strategy design, and implementation.

One of the key importance of The Seventh Buddhist Council, and the urgency to implement it, is because the 21st Century will perhaps be the only century for Buddhism, as far as public and private policy at the local, national, regional, and global levels are concerned.

Thus, it has become a true moral mandate to present and to share the Social Teachings of the Buddha, in ways that everyone may understand and apply them (e.g., trade, wealth, poverty, rights, livelihood, environment, gender).

Today, there is a tremendous decay in our civilization. The material progress of this civilization has always been supported by a powerful Social Doctrine, which is the one that justifies different forms of material wealth; its creation, accumulation, concentration, as well as the social values and ethics that accompany those processes. Today, this civilization has failed, creating a huge gap that is to be filled right now.

- This is happening in both East and West.

- The fundamental question is whose spiritual foundation will fill the gap.

- We must open a door to bring all Buddha's teachings to bear on this gap.

- People are demanding answers.

- A Buddhist Social Doctrine is to fill this gap.

A new social doctrine must emerge from the council. The content and the path towards filling this gap will also determine the future of Buddhism and of most congregations in the world. If we do not provide answers to the issues facing humanity, there is very little future for Buddhism.

JUSTIFICATION FOR A SEVENTH BUDDHIST COUNCIL

In the same way that "social doctrines" of other spiritual or religious communities have substantially influenced and dominated (in relative terms) other centuries of human existence—e.g., their powerful influences on economics, politics, business, environment, ecology, sustainability, social, institutional, governance, human rights—it seems clear that this is the time of Buddhism. The teachings, ideas, and understandings embedded in the Buddha's human, community, and social doctrine now form a robust body of thoughts, concepts, actions, policies, and implementable programs necessary to address almost all the issues and problems humanity faces in this 21st Century. This would be at the center of the Seventh Buddhist Council.

The Seventh Buddhist Council should address how to bring forth openly the Buddha's social teachings. The absence of this Buddhist Social Doctrine (BSD) within the practices of daily human activities is due mainly to: (i) a lack of knowledge by decision- and policy-makers alike; (ii) a misunderstanding of the boundaries of the Buddha's teachings; or simply (iii) a disregard for what the Buddha taught in relation to the attributes and problems of our daily social livelihood, collective behavior, and societal efforts.

Today, there is a misguided impression that the Buddha only taught about personal inner unfoldment and about how to expand individually-tailored human consciousness attainments. There is this idea that everything in Buddhism is only about individual enlightenment arising from a set of practices, initiations, realizations, the power of silence, inner healing, change in habits, abstentions, merits, and not about collective enlightenment. This emphasis has led to focusing quasi-exclusively on the individual aspects of Buddhism.

The Seventh Buddhist Council will share the fact that some of the main causes and conditions of suffering are social and collective in nature (something also expressed above). Social suffering is a key ingredient of 21st-century societies.

Examples of this social suffering abound. Just think about COVID-19, climate change, biodiversity depletion, instability and insecurity, social and ecological migration, exclusion and marginalization, violation of human and nature rights, war and conflicts, inadequate health policies and services, lack of education, poor water and sewerage systems, moral and ethical vacuums, etc.

Today, it is almost impossible to separate individual suffering from collective suffering. There are no boundaries any longer. This absence of boundaries becomes more evident when one tries to define and assign key shared responsibilities for what is happening in the world today.

> **Examples of social suffering abound**

Once again, the Seventh Buddhist Council will draw upon the direct teachings of the Buddha, as expressed within a large number of Sutras and Vinaya. Perhaps, this is its single most important contribution, enabling humanity to benefit from a Buddhist Social Doctrine. This Doctrine will be greatly influenced by the values of generosity, cooperation, interdependence, mutuality, love, compassion, justice, rights, trust, equanimity, rigor, and more.

SPECIFIC ASPECTS TO CONSIDER

The Seventh Buddhist Council, via the Buddha's social teachings and a Global Vinaya, will:

I.   *Establish the basis for a coherent and balanced livelihood.* These social teachings will influence the areas of economics (wealth and welfare), politics (political leadership), institutions (community organizations), social (policies and programs), business, governance, human rights, sustainable development, environment, etc.

II.   *Make the Buddha's Social Teachings universally accessible on all continents:* (i) to create the networking conditions necessary to empower policymakers through new forms of collective-spiritual-wisdom, (ii) to construct a harmonious planetary livelihood, and (iii) to alleviate human individual and social suffering through the enhanced power of collective consciousness. Once again, it is a commitment to create a "Global Vinaya."

III.   *Suggest alternative paths to move humanity from the current paradigm of "individual materialism" into inner-conscious societies.* The Seventh Buddhist Council, through Buddha's social wisdom and practices—still very relevant for the challenges we face in this 21st Century—will spiritually reconnect private and public, inner and outer, material and non-material, individual and collective economics, politics, business, and institutions.

IV.   *Be committed to the construction and emergence of a new collective reality.* This would be based on a different set of values, ethics, and principles, so that human beings, sentient beings, and nature attain their full potential. From all of the above, new narratives will emerge, which will deeply change the process of transformation of human beings, sentient beings, and nature.

V.   *Focus on preserving and verifying the teachings of the Buddha, including the Dhamma and Vinaya.* It should address any discrepancies or inconsistencies in the existing Buddhist scriptures and clarify any misunderstood teachings. It should strive to promote unity and harmony among different Buddhist traditions and schools by finding common ground and resolving doctrinal differences. The Council should explore ways to adapt and disseminate the Buddhist teachings in the modern world, considering cultural, social, and technologi-

> **The Seventh Buddhist Council will draw upon the direct teachings of the Buddha**

cal changes. It should emphasize the importance of ethical conduct, mindfulness, and compassion as core values of Buddhism.

VI.   *Address contemporary issues such as environmental sustainability, social justice, and peace-building from a Buddhist perspective.* It should promote dialogue and understanding among different religious traditions and foster interfaith cooperation for the common good. The Council should also (as always) encourage the study and practice of meditation as a means to cultivate inner peace, wisdom, and spiritual growth. It should renew its support to the education and training of monks, nuns, and lay practitioners in Buddhist teachings and practices. It should explore ways to make Buddhist teachings more accessible to a wider audience, including through digital platforms and online resources.

VII.   *Focus, once again, on the role of women in Buddhism and work towards gender equality and inclusivity within the monastic community.* It should address issues of social inequality, poverty, and discrimination, and explore ways in which Buddhism can contribute to positive social change. It must promote environmental awareness and sustainable living practices based on Buddhist principles of interdependence and compassion for all beings. It should address the challenges of globalization and consumerism and explore ways to promote simplicity, contentment, and mindful consumption. It should support efforts to preserve and protect sacred Buddhist sites, artifacts, and cultural heritage for future generations.

VIII.   *Promote dialogue and reconciliation* in regions affected by conflict or violence, drawing on Buddhist teachings of nonviolence and compassion. It should address issues of mental health and well-being, and explore how Buddhist practices such as mindfulness and loving-kindness can support emotional resilience and psychological healing. The Council has to promote research and scholarship in Buddhist studies, encouraging the translation and publication of Buddhist texts and academic exchange among scholars. It ought to address the challenges of religious extremism and fundamentalism, promoting a more inclusive and tolerant understanding of Buddhism that respects diversity and pluralism.

IX. *Inspire and empower Buddhists and non-Buddhists around the world* to live according to the values of wisdom, compassion, and ethical conduct, contributing to a more peaceful and harmonious society.

X. *Be organized around promoting peace and nonviolence* as core values of Buddhist teachings and advocating for conflict resolution through dialogue and reconciliation; addressing social inequality and poverty by supporting initiatives that promote economic justice, access to education, and healthcare for marginalized communities; advocating for human rights and social justice by speaking out against discrimination, oppression, and injustice in all its forms; and supporting environmental sustainability and conservation efforts to protect the planet and promote a harmonious relationship with nature.

XI. *Encourage ethical leadership and governance* based on principles of integrity, transparency, and accountability in both the public and private sectors; foster interfaith dialogue and cooperation to promote understanding, tolerance, and peaceful coexistence among different religious communities; advocate gender equality and women's rights within the Buddhist community and society at large; support initiatives that promote mental health and well-being through mindfulness, meditation, and psychological support; address the challenges of globalization and consumerism by promoting ethical consumption, sustainability, and mindful living; and advocate the rights of refugees, migrants, and displaced persons, supporting efforts to provide humanitarian assistance and protection to those in need.

XII. *Promote education and literacy among disadvantaged populations,* including children, women, and marginalized communities; support initiatives that promote social harmony, cultural diversity, and mutual respect among different ethnic and religious groups; advocate for the protection of human rights, freedom of expression, and the rule of law in societies where these values are under threat; support efforts to combat corruption, bribery, and unethical practices in government, business, and civil society; promote initiatives that address the root causes of violence, extremism, and radicalization through education, dialogue, and community engagement; advocate for the rights of indigenous peoples and support efforts to protect their land, culture, and heritage; and support initiatives that promote sustainable agriculture, food security, and access to clean water for all.

XIII. *Foster partnerships with governments, international organizations, and civil society* to address global challenges such as climate change, poverty, and inequality; to implement human rights acceptance, inclusion, and equality for all; and promote civic engagement, social responsibility, and active citizenship among Buddhists, encouraging them to contribute to the common good and social welfare of their communities.

Chapter 3:

IMPLEMENTING SOCIAL TEACHINGS OF THE BUDDHA: KING ASHOKA

"All men are my children. All should live here happily and benefit. (...) All men that they should obtain it (happiness). May last long as (my) sons and great-grandsons as long as the moon and the sun."

King Ashoka

The Emperor Ashoka was the first one to implement the Social Teachings of the Buddha, kingdom-wise. In particular, to focus on macro policies and forms of governance based on Buddhism proper. Even though this kingdom took place many centuries ago, its societal paradigm and experience are still useful to the present situation of our world. Naturally, there is a need for modifications and validation to apply to our circumstances.

This chapter illustrates the first practical application of social Buddhist solutions to humanity's challenges and problems. The geographic and cultural focus here is on ancient India (the unification of India) during the reign of Emperor Ashoka. The most interesting conclusion after studying the policies adopted in that kingdom is that situational evaluation was as relevant then as it is now. Clearly, one must understand the differences in today's local context.

ASHOKA'S BUDDHIST ECONOMICS AND POLITICS

Thus, the emphasis in this presentation is more on breadth than depth. Total comprehensiveness is beyond the scope of this chapter. This chapter was originally drafted as a teaching device. It neither intends to be comprehensive nor to enter the many controversial dimensions of that era in human history. The original idea was to create incentives among readers so that they are inclined to select one or more themes addressed here (e.g., economics, governance, public policy, social integration, education, public goods) and decide to "specialize" (deepen) on that particular theme from a Buddhist perspective. This exercise is very relevant for gaining culture and essential knowledge about possible forms of integrating Buddhist solutions into today's world situation.

This chapter possesses a mix of materials from several readings, as well as from artificial intelligence. The latter became useful and relevant to be able to "broom" through a huge chunk of literature. The key here is how one poses "questions" to AI during this inquiry and sifts through the most relevant materials.

ABOUT ASHOKA

Ashoka (meaning "the one without sorrow"), also known as "Ashoka the Great," was an ancient Indian emperor of the Maurya Dynasty, who ruled from 268 to 232 BCE. By many scholars, Ashoka the Great is considered one of India's greatest emperors and a significant figure in world history. Military conquests marked Ashoka's reign, but, after a brutal war in Kalinga, he experienced a profound change of inner direction and spiritual path; a major spiritual awakening about choosing the path of non-violence.

"His majesty feels remorse, sorrow, and regret on account of the conquest because of the slaughter, death, and people taken captive — The loss of a hundredth or thousandth part of those slaughtered or carried away would now be a matter of deep regret..."

He embraced Buddhism and, based on that, designed and implemented many public policies centered on non-violence, tolerance, and the welfare of all forms of life, not just human beings. As part of his policy and institutional package, Ashoka promoted religious and cultural diversity and freedom (a series of social and cultural human rights), constructed numerous public monuments (some aimed at communicating his policies and narratives widely), and established a network of hospitals and universities (the establishment of important public goods).

He also implemented policies regarding poverty alleviation (understanding the relationship between poverty and spiritual development) and animal rights and protection (recognizing sentient beings as part and parcel of social policymaking). He was famous for his edicts (a unique form of strategic communication), inscribed on rocks and pillars, which provided valuable insights into his governance and moral teachings—that is, an instrument of public communication and dissemination. In the end, he left a legacy perceived by a large majority as a compassionate and visionary ruler, with lasting impacts on Indian history and society (particularly the unification of the Indian continent).

SOME OF ASHOKA'S BUDDHIST HISTORY-BASED POLICIES

There are several examples of how Ashoka constructed a Social Doctrine by "translating" the social teachings of the Buddha into public policymaking. In today's world, one may think about the Kingdom of Bhutan as another example (measuring human welfare via "Gross National Happiness" instead of "Gross National Product"). To Ashoka, Buddhism provided the scaffold of a right view for the future of every person and sentient being within the kingdom. Let us list a few examples of those policies:

Promoted the Principle of Non-Violence (Ahimsa).

While his history as emperor began full of violence, once he converted to Buddhism, he shifted into a path of non-violence. He promoted the principle of non-violence and compassion towards all living beings, and as a way to disseminate this approach, emphasized the importance of respecting and protecting all forms of life, including animals. In today's terminology, he implemented a strong biodiversity protection and management policy.

Supported the Buddhist Community Everywhere (Sangha).

The government provided patronage to Buddhist monks and nuns (adoption and maintenance of the monastic societies), offering them protection, resources, and land for the construction of monasteries (provision of the initial capital stock—something still prevailing in many countries of the world). He also sponsored the sending of "Buddhist Missions" (including sending his own son to Sri Lanka) to spread the teachings of the Buddha to different countries and regions in Asia and beyond.

Constructed Many Stupas and Pillars (Dharma).

Ashoka erected numerous stupas (dome-shaped structures containing relics) and pillars with inscriptions detailing his commitment to Dhamma (the truth, essence of righteousness) and the promotion of moral values. This was a form of "social media" for that time in history. These constructions were also Ashoka's way to keep the kingdom united, to promote his presence in faraway places (Greece, Afghanistan), and to disseminate Buddhist teachings, morality, and wisdom. It became an innovative and powerful instrument to do so. One of the most famous of these pillars is the one he constructed in Sarnath (near the city of Varanasi), which emphasized the fact that it was the sacred place where the Buddha delivered his First Sermon. Also, within this context, one should note that Ashoka built edicts with the sole purpose of teaching the Dharma, which included, for example, some unique moral instructions for his communities, advocating religious tolerance, sharing his social welfare measures, and promoting harmony and non-violence.
Narratives in Some of the Pillars. "To observe the moral rule. Individuals have been put in prison undeservedly. You must be at hand to stop unwarranted imprisonment and torture." "The advancement of social

ethics amongst men has been achieved by legislation, and I consider how I may bring happiness to the people, not only to relatives of mine or residents of my capital city, but also to those who are far removed from me. I act in the same manner with respect to all. I am concerned similarly with all classes. But I consider it my principal duty to visit the people personally."

Designed Several Important Welfare Measures (Vinaya). He was deeply involved in improving the welfare of the collective. Thus, his policies, incentives, investments, and institutional reforms focused on several important public goods. In particular, he implemented welfare measures for his people everywhere, including the establishment of hospitals, veterinary clinics, and rest houses for travelers (and mendicants). He also encouraged the planting of trees and the digging of wells for the benefit of the community. Thus, interventions were included to attain a sustainable society in ecological and social grounds.

Promoted Cultural Exchange (Social Ethics). In such a diverse kingdom, it was necessary to establish and promote many forms of cultural exchanges in a mutual fashion, and to create the needed incentives for different religious and philosophical traditions to engage in relevant dialogues and not in discriminating and sectarian acts of aggression (promote an "ecumenical" view of the kingdom). Thus, his government respected all religious beliefs and encouraged non-discrimination, tolerance, and understanding among its diverse communities. This was a way to commit to many moral values, forms of effective social welfare, restraint from violence, and promote socially relevant Buddhist teachings throughout his empire. He left a true legacy as a Buddhist monarch, establishing a peaceful and humane governance.

DETAILS OF VARIOUS ASHOKA'S EDICTS

The inscription of Ashoka's edicts—not only in India but in many countries of Asia—was widespread. The purpose of this section is to bring most of the edicts to the modern policy decision-making frameworks and, thus, understand their usefulness to resolve many of humanity's social, economic, political, and institutional problems. Their wide geographic distribution meant that many of the edicts were found written in many different languages. This was an intrinsic characteristic of Ashoka's communication strategy. Some of the edicts are written in Greek! This demonstrates how far Buddhism spread in its early life. Bilingual edicts were also found in Afghanistan.

> **The Edicts as an instrument of governance**

The edicts have been classified archaeologically into several categories: 14 major rock edicts, two minor rock edicts, seven major pillar edicts, a minor pillar edict, inscriptions on the Barabar Hills, and commemorative inscriptions (Ashoka's opinions). However, no one has classified them within a framework of country policies.

The following is an example of the possible applications of what Ashoka did to the present situation facing humanity. For that, attention will be paid to the Major Rock Edicts, knowing that the same could be done for other edicts (major and minor pillar edicts). The Major Rocks were chosen because they give a pretty good idea of "How to Govern the State."

MAJOR ROCK EDICTS

I: Biodiversity Conservation and Animal Protection: It prohibits the killing of animals and prohibits animal cruelty.

II: Inclusive Social and Economic Policies for Rural Development: community development through people's protection, the digging of water wells for the use of humans and animals, providing medical services to humans and animals, the growing of medicinal plants and fruits, and the provision of medical care for people and animals.

III: Dharma-Based Form of Governance: ruling the functions of government representatives at different levels for the dissemination of the Dharma, including business and morality-related issues, establishing what was meritorious and unwholesome, and respect for certain people in society (Brahmins).

IV: Principles of Non-Violence: the proclamation of the right speech based on Dharma, the proclamation of the sound of morality and the practice of merits (boon), and not war and conflict, to maximize the positive impacts of Dharma in society.

V: Human Rights and Dissemination of the Dharma: commencing with the practice of virtuous deeds, followed by pointing specifically to the existence of slaves and their treatment—under the human rights principle that "Every human is my child"—as well as defining the important role of the Dhamma Mahamatras who are those who disseminate the social teachings of the Buddha, with particular emphasis on ethics and morality.

VI: Announcing the importance of grassroots development (knowing what is happening in the field) and asserting that one of the most important duties of a king was the welfare of his people.

VII: The Human Right of Non-Discrimination and Freedom of Religion: with special preoccupation for self-control and purity of the mind, recognizing the problems sectarianism would bring, such as diminishing the capacity to unite the empire through Buddhism, creating religious discrimination everywhere, and promoting gratitude and self-control.

VIII: Human Welfare through Practicing the Dharma: referring to the importance of Dharma Yatra as the path to happiness via the Dharma or truth in the wisdom of the Five Precepts; establishing the so-called torus of morality, assisting the aged and other members of society, and preserving important aspects of livelihood and education.

IX: Avoiding the Wrong Path: with special emphasis on those rituals and useless or doubtful ceremonies practiced at the time, which move people away from the true Buddhist Dharma, in response to superstitions, wrong shamanism, and the sacrifice of sentient beings.

X: Moving from Egocentric Policies to Dharma Policies: denouncing those acts and behaviors leading to expanded fame and glory for the sake of status and social imposition, and focusing on merits through the practice of Dharma—the Dharma of the other (not accepting spiritual status as a mirror of a given social status).

XI: The Power of Wisdom and Social Stability: indicating the importance of being meritorious by "distributing morality," including respect for senior citizens and their wisdom, kindness to family and friends, as well as propagating love and compassion to sentient beings.

XII: The Importance of Tolerance: particularly religious tolerance in a continent with various forms of faith and religious practices, fundamental to any system of human rights, and guarding for the right speech always.

XIII: Peace and No War: as a policy to establish a society at the center of the mandala, irradiating Dharma principles and avoiding the brutality of war; embracing the study of morality, love of morality, and the instruction of people in morality—i.e., building the bridges from chaos to peace.

XIV: The Power of Narratives: those narratives based on the teachings of the Buddha, disseminated all over the kingdom, and made explicit to everyone in the kingdom.

BUDDHIST HISTORICAL PRINCIPLES OF INTERVENTION

As we can see from above, after his conversion to Buddhism, Emperor Ashoka's actions were deeply influenced by Buddhist principles and his commitment to the Buddha's teachings. There is a clear correlation of these policies with many specific Sutras of the Buddha. Compared to previous kings, he reigned by implementing a large number of "benevolent policies," a concept we should consider in today's world.

Also, the reader will note that such principles are highly correlated with the attributes of so-called "Buddhist Solutions," in relation to **"Non-Buddhist Solutions":**

The Promotion of Non-Violence (Ahimsa): This may sound easy and repetitive, but for an emperor who was known for violent governance (e.g., the brutal Kalinga War), it was not trivial to embrace the principle of non-violence. As stated earlier, he issued edicts promoting compassion and respect for all living beings, including animals. Thus, non-violence was established for all forms and manifestations of life.

The Strengthening and Empowerment of Communities, including the Buddhist Sangha: As part of public policymaking, part of the national budget was allocated to provide patronage to Buddhist monks and nuns, including offering them protection, material resources, and land for monastery construction. His government also sponsored the sending of Buddhist missions to spread Buddhist teachings to different regions.

The Practice of Buddhist Right Behavior and Effort: Important promotion of moral values and social welfare principles based on righteousness. Emphasized virtues such as truthfulness, kindness, humility, and respect for elders.

The Respect for Human Rights: Central for the new India he helped shape. Part of these rights included religious tolerance, not a minor principle, now enshrined in the Universal Declaration of Human Rights. Ashoka respected and supported various religious traditions, promoting harmony among diverse subjects.

The Power of Cultural Exchange as a Form of Integration and Union: The essential principle was to promote cultural exchange and intellectual dialogue, fostering a climate of learning and knowledge-sharing. He sponsored the spread of Buddhist teachings and supported preservation of ancient texts and scriptures.

Ethical and Moral Governance: By committing to various Buddhist principles (non-violence, compassion, social welfare, moral and ethical values, religious tolerance, peace, and cultural exchange), Ashoka established ethical governance. He appointed ombudsmen (Dharma Mahamatras) to prevent wrongful imprisonment or chastisement and to remove hindrances and deliver justice, especially in cases involving large families or calamities.

ECONOMICS AND GOVERNANCE: YET ANOTHER ANGLE

Ashoka also made significant contributions in the economic and administrative spheres.

Economic Policies:
Agricultural Development: Promoted agricultural and rural development by encouraging the cultivation of crops, particularly herbs and fruit trees, and the construction of irrigation systems (e.g., wells for humans and animals).

Trade and Commerce:
Facilitated trade by improving transportation networks, building roads, and establishing trade routes within the empire. Explicitly stated that what the kingdom did not have had to be produced or imported. Promoted trade relations with neighboring regions and facilitated cultural exchange through commerce.

Monetary System:
Introduced standardized weights and measures across the empire to regulate trade and ensure fair economic transactions (Fair Trade System). Issued coins with inscriptions promoting Dhamma (righteousness) and ethical conduct.

Taxation System:
Implemented a unique taxation system to finance government operations and welfare activities (modern concept of balancing the budget). Taxes were levied on agricultural produce, trade transactions, and other revenue sources.

Governance-Related Policies:

• *Administrative Reforms:* Introduced reforms to streamline governance and improve efficiency. Decentralized the public administration system, dividing the empire into provinces with appointed officials overseeing local administration.

• *A Powerful and Fair Judicial System:* Established a judicial system based on fairness and justice, inclusive of all social classes, including slaves. Emphasized impartiality, compassion, and adherence to the rule of law.

• *Social and Economic Welfare Measures:* Implemented measures impacting welfare directly, including hospitals, veterinary clinics, support for the elderly, disabled, and disadvantaged. Regular censuses collected data, including caste and occupation.

• *Promotion of Religious Tolerance:* Though not strictly economic or governmental, religious tolerance was essential for peace and security. Economic interventions' effectiveness also depended on policies of religious tolerance and respect for all faiths, contributing to social harmony and unity.

"...man must not do reverence to his own sect by disparaging that of another for trivial reasons. Other people's sects deserve reverence. By acting in this way, a man exalts his own sect and at the same time does service to the sects of other people."

• *Environmental Conservation:* Ethical governance reflected a deep concern for environmental conservation and sustainable development. Promoted planting trees, digging wells, and wildlife protection.

• *The Power of Respect:* Emphasized respect in addressing human and social issues. Examples include tolerance of other religions and spiritual paths; humane treatment of slaves and servants; progressive elimination of conflict through Buddhist Dharma; obedience and respect to parents, adults, teachers, and monks; abolition of the death sentence; prohibition of killing animals; digging wells; building rest houses; planting trees; and helping those in poverty.

ON ETHICAL GOVERNANCE

The concept of "ethical governance" was supported by Buddha's teachings, based on the principle of righteousness. The strength of ethical governance came from emphasis on moral values, compassion, non-violence, and social welfare. Ashoka's legacy as an ethical ruler continues to inspire leaders and policymakers worldwide. His example serves as a model for governing with compassion, integrity, and commitment to the well-being of all citizens. His edicts offer valuable insights into principles of modern ethical governance and the importance of upholding moral values in leadership.

The greatness of Ashoka was the ethic dictated by Dharma about the use of force and violence, as he practiced before his conversion to Buddhism. Also, the importance he gave to the reconciliation of economics and spirituality, i.e., material and spiritual welfare; reconciliation among social rights and shared responsibilities; and the embrace of social ethics towards all manifestations of life.

ADDITIONAL INTERPRETATION OF ASHOKA'S ECONOMICS AND GOVERNANCE

There was a major attention paid to the themes of administration, public management, and economy. Three fundamental pillars of any notion of political economy in the 21st century. The three of them a unique character and content, and a specific institutional framework to implement them. In practice, they were collected through the design and implementation of benevolent investment, policies, and organizational structures. As part of the paternalistic narrative of the government, Ashoka declared that

"All men are my children".

The above approach demanded that the king be always well-informed to assist all people. He had a network of so-called Pativedakas, or reporters; an essential part of the scaffold of decision-making, which is very absent today. This was accompanied by administrative actions, including, for example, a census and occupational surveys to reflect reality on the ground. This was strengthened by a successful economy, quite export-oriented. Also, there was a keen awareness of the need for public revenues to finance the demanded public goods like health (human health and animal health), transport, parks, nature reserves, education, construction of temples, highways, and transport. However, at the core of all of this paradigm was the aim of attaining the highest level of well-being of human beings and sentient beings.

There was a major attention to the material economy. Economy and spirituality were at the forefront of policy and decision-making by the empire. Many of us have seen the initial seed of Buddhist Economics in Ashoka's kingdom. But, this economics could not be practiced within an ethical vacuum. The social teachings of the Buddha were essential ingredients in this form of economy, within which "more was not necessarily better".

This form of economy was intertwined with humanitarian and ethical governance. This seems to be the "magic formula" for a society to prosper within a recognized cross-cultural-religious society. Ashoka was aware of the fact that the Buddha met many political and economic leaders during his time. Examples of them are the kings Bimbisara and King Pasenadi; many Suttas account for their productive relationship.

All the above could not have been done without a very special form of conscious leadership. There are many accounts about what constitutes leadership. However, Ashoka was probably aware of the essence expressed in The Cakkavatti Sutta, which states four main ingredients of good leadership: upholding righteousness, caring for the well-being of all people, being protective, being fair (just), trust, and integrity. It is not about ego or thirst for power, as expressed in The Agganna Sutta.

It was not just a matter of expertise, but of a true moral conduct and governing with generosity, benevolence, paternalism, and compassion. To do so, one had to be deeply engaged in humanistic virtues. Ashoka had some notion of a society with a clear moral standard (non-violence, non-discrimination, respect, and appropriate rituals), based on the Dharma.

No less important was Ashoka's interest in the environment and social sustainability. It promoted the digging of wells, crucial to developing agriculture. Animal care and health were central in cities and rural areas. Economic and social support to the needy and the elderly people (the essence of a social security policy for the kingdom).

Ashoka was completely aware of the importance of human rights and shared responsibilities. As the empire grew in size, it also grew in cultural and religious complexity, and free expression became fundamental. Animal Rights also became prominent. He was capable of making Dharma his civil ideology.

Chapter 4:

NATURE OF BUDDHIST SOLUTIONS

"How wonderful will it be when all beings experience each other as limbs on the one body of life."

Shantideva

PURPOSE AND INTRODUCTION

This chapter contains some examples of the possible dimensions of what constitutes a "Buddhist Solution" to the issues and problems humanity faces today. What we know now is that the majority of the solutions, which have been tried around the world, have yet to yield the expected results, or their results are not long-lived or sustainable. Thus, new types of solutions are needed. The material presented here is the fruit of many years of studies and experience in socio-economic development and ex-post evaluation of projects and programs at the country and regional levels.

The first step requires the identification of some essential "attributes" of what constitutes a Buddhist Solution and the acknowledgment of what is contained in the available Sutras. It is important to note that there is a correlation between the nature and scope of Buddhist

Solutions and the fundamentals of a Buddhist Social Doctrine. Thus, the reader needs to reflect upon which one, out of all the suggestions presented here, will serve as a vehicle to better understand the various steps required to construct **"A Buddhist Social Doctrine."** A Buddhist Social Doctrine will map into solutions, and Buddhist Solutions will contribute to consolidating a Buddhist Social Doctrine. One has to work on both fronts at the same time. Otherwise, the future scenarios are rather gloomy.

ATTRIBUTES OF A BUDDHIST SOLUTION

Let us start with a fundamental question: What are the relevant ingredients, attributes, and characteristics of a Buddhist Solution?

Here are some key aspects that make those ingredients stand out:

A. *Acknowledging the Importance of Interconnectedness and Interdependence:* Buddhist teachings emphasize the interconnectedness and interdependence of all beings and phenomena. We are not independent and separate entities (islands). The holistic view that emerges from an interdependent world validates a sense of unity in diversity and mutuality and cooperation in addressing today's world problems. What this says is that all decisions or actions affect many beings over both space and time. Space relates to the fact that what happens in one part of the planet affects people all over the planet. Examples are global warming, climate change, spread of diseases (COVID-19), attrition of biodiversity, pollution of oceans and rivers. A Buddhist solution recognizes the power of interdependence.This is an essential statement when defining what is considered a Buddhist solution. The social doctrine today emphasizes independence, separability, and exclusion.

B. *Embracing Non-Violence and Compassion:* Buddhism promotes non-violence (ahimsa) and compassion towards all sentient beings. Also, the self-realization of compassion as well as the construction of a compassionate society. This principle of non-violence is central to policy-making in all aspects of life, and to resolving conflicts and promoting harmony at a planetary scale. There are many forms of violence (physical, verbal), and we must make sure that the proposed solutions do not lead to more violence and conflict. Today, some solutions embody violence, both in the medium and longer term. This includes violence to human beings, sentient beings, and nature. The ecological disaster we witness today shows that many of the solutions are violent to nature. There are many examples of violence against nature; e.g., the demise of natural forests, the depletion of biodiversity, various forms of air and water pollution, sacrifice and violence against animals, etc. The chapter about the Buddha's views on environment and sustainable development enlarges this discussion.

C. *Emphasizing Ethics and Morality*: Buddhism places a strong emphasis on ethical conduct and moral values at the individual and collective levels. In the social teachings of the Buddha, ethics provides the foundation and counterbalance in the creation of material wealth and its distribution. These ethical considerations are to become the preconditions for any Buddhist solutions proposed. Specifically, decision-making must not be exercised within a moral and ethical vacuum. By promoting ethical behavior and virtuous right actions, Buddhist solutions aim at creating a more harmonious, equitable, and just planetary society. Let us be aware of the importance of both the individual and social dimensions of ethics and morals. In the chapters related to human rights, there is a discussion about the importance of an ethical foundation when defining jurisprudence and the justiciability of rights and shared responsibilities. The presence of this ethical foundation becomes the needed ingredient to understand, define, and apply human rights.

D. *Emphasizing the Self-Realization of Inner Peace*: Buddhism emphasizes deriving world peace from inner peace and the practice of mindfulness. Thus, any Buddhist solution must account for and be embedded in our inner transformation and personal development. The human path is not just about more materiality. This is why Buddhist solutions often, if not always, aim at addressing the root causes of suffering and conflict; rather often situations within humanity today. Solutions that do not embody inner peace and social peace must be scrutinized thoroughly. Self-realization is one of the trademarks in Buddhism; thus, to make a conscious decision to go inside and not define points of reference that are merely attached to our outside human reality. As His Holiness Lama Gangchen Rinpoche taught humanity: *"Inner peace is the most solid foundation of world peace."*

E. *Mindfulness and Awareness:* Buddhism makes us aware that most of its ingrained solutions embody a state of the mind (individual and collective)—a level of refinement of the mind—that correlates with that decision and the expected results. Thus, the importance of meditation and individual inner development and transformation is within all possible solutions. Meditation will ensure the quality of our solutions and the amount of expected beneficial impacts. Buddhist practices such as meditation and mindfulness (sati) help individuals develop a heightened awareness of their thoughts, emotions, and actions. This heightened awareness can lead to more conscious decision-making, conscious leadership, conscious governance, and a greater sense of shared rights and responsibility towards the world. Buddhist solutions and their supporting values will create the conditions for a true holistic approach to resolving world problems. It is imperative to reach the transcendental state of human reality, rooted in the human mind (citta), wisdom *(prajñā)*, and consciousness *(viññāṇa)*.

It is essential to know a rule of spiritual understanding of reality: every aspect of life (solution) that surges has a perfect correlate with a very specific level of human consciousness. Thus, as we prepare Buddhist solutions, these must be linked to that level of consciousness we are seeking at any moment in time.

WHAT MAKES THE DIFFERENCE?

Within this context, there are several key differences among alternative solutions. Examples of these are:

I. *Root Cause vs. Symptom Treatment:* Buddhist solutions focus on addressing the root causes and conditions and not just the external symptoms. This is why the state of the mind and the level of consciousness are decision variables in those solutions. The choice of solutions is intimately related to the individual and collective inner states of being. More often than not, there is a high correlation between the choices made and the solutions proposed with the state of the mind; i.e., a clear mind, clear solutions. In contrast, many modern solutions tend to focus on treating the symptoms or external manifestations of problems without addressing the underlying causes. Frequently, the state of the mind and human consciousness are not relevant variables. Thus, we end up looking for solutions with the consciousness that was responsible for the problem in the first place. One needs to pay attention to the root causes and not just look for palliatives that will address manifestations of the challenges and issues involved. This theme is not trivial, as one is confronted with the paradox of consciousness: **"We are not aware that we are not aware."** Thus, new solutions need higher awareness and more clarity in the mind to solve the problems at hand.

II. *Emphasis on Inner Transformation:* Inner transformation is an input and an outcome of the cycle of problems and solutions. The solutions proposed today are not anchored in the goal of human, sentient beings, and nature's transformation in their maximum expression. We are fully aware that the solutions we have proposed to date are leading to negative transformation of the mind, body, and soul. Thus, Buddhist solutions often emphasize that the beginning of any process of decision-making starts with the identification of the relevance of "inner transformation" and "personal development" as a means to resolve problems. This is not an esoteric or abstract proposition. The transformation of any society begins with the inner transformation of the individuals living in that society. This is why solutions must be accompanied by those instruments that transform the mind and body, like involving the practices of meditation, mindfulness, and self-reflection. Furthermore, most solutions demand or involve some process of self-realization. This is particularly important when addressing issues of justice, human rights, shared responsibilities, equity, and cooperation. All of these are now essential in a totally interdependent human civilization. We are bound to cultivate the qualities and values of compassion, wisdom, love, truth, joy, and equanimity. In contrast, modern solutions often prioritize external material interventions only, such as policy changes, investment implementation, technological advancements, market intervention, and institutional development. Buddhist solutions always try to establish the **"inner seeds"** of any solution proposed. This is not a common practice today.

This is essential in Buddhism. The level of refinement of the mind and human consciousness is not an exogenous variable in the search for solutions. As stated later on in this paragraph, in the traditional paradigm of solutions, mind and consciousness are not even considered relevant.

Today, there is a duality between inner development and outer development. They are seen as two separate worlds. The Buddha taught us the Law of Correspondence, which states that the inner is like the outer and the outer is like the inner. Two inseparable realities. Perhaps the most fundamental decision in our spiritual path has to do with entering the stream of our inner self.

III. *Again–Non-Violence and Compassion:* This issue is brought here once again, as there are many forms of veiled or explicit violence. It is not only about the physical aggression one may experience from another person. There is violence in economics, politics, business, and the like. As with the Four Noble Truths, the first thing policymakers have to do is To Know the Truth of Violence. Without knowing this truth, it is impossible to identify and select the causes and conditions of violence in all its expressions. The path to the elimination of violence passes through understanding it fully.

Generally speaking, Buddhist solutions advocate for non-violence, compassion, love, joy, equanimity, and empathy as fundamental principles in addressing people's problems. But how are they embodied in any solution? In some cases, the answer is not evident, as it needs individual and collective action. We also know from "The Four Noble Truths" that the second path to resolving world problems is the practice of virtues. The public mechanisms and options are not many. The neatest one is education and other forms of human development. These have become more part of the problem than part of the solution. The practice of these virtues is central, for example, to address conflict resolution, social justice, and community development. While modern solutions may also value these virtues, they may sometimes prioritize them differently or to a lesser extent. The average person on the streets will often say that we are dominated by greed and ego, and that the solutions proposed promote more greed and ego.

IV. *Holistic and/or Fragmented Solutions:* It is easy to say that today's solutions are not holistic. But some Buddhist solutions may also be fragmented in nature. The relevant point here is to determine when such a solution is holistic. What should be within the container that will make a solution holistic? Solutions cannot contain everything, as they become non-implementable or inefficient in addressing the problem that justifies such a solution. Thus, what are the types of components that contribute to a Buddhist holistic solution?

Dictionary.com states that: **"Holistic"** is an adjective that describes things related to the idea that the whole is more than the sum of its parts. In other words, the entirety of something must be considered instead of just considering its parts.

To be **"more than the sum of the parts"**, Buddhist solutions to addressing problems consider a series of laws and principles, which are fundamental to all manifestations of life. Lord Buddha is very explicit in the teaching of these laws.

Here are some of these key spiritual laws or principles:

1. THE LAW OF KARMA:

Karma is the law of cause and effect, and the law of infinite equilibrium (harmony) in Buddhism. It states that our actions have consequences (i.e., all our decisions have karmic effects, as there are very few that are karmic neutral), and that positive actions lead to positive outcomes, while negative actions lead to negative outcomes. By understanding the law of karma, individuals can take responsibility for their actions and cultivate virtuous behavior. This is perhaps one of the most important Buddhist laws as regards instruments and solutions to world problems.

2. THE LAW OF INTERDEPENDENCE:

Buddhism emphasizes the interconnectedness and interdependence of all beings and phenomena, as stated above. This law teaches that all things are interconnected and that our actions have ripple effects that impact the world around us. By recognizing our interdependence, individuals can cultivate compassion and empathy for all living beings.

3. THE LAW OF NON-SELF:

Buddhism teaches the concept of non-self (anatta), which challenges the idea of a fixed and permanent self. This law emphasizes the impermanent and ever-changing nature of the self, leading to a deeper understanding of the nature of reality and the interconnectedness of all beings.

4. THE LAW OF CORRESPONDENCE:

Buddhism emphasizes the relationships that exist between our inner ecology, including the mind, and the outer ecology, including nature. There are several inter-connecting points, the most important of which are the five elements of life: water, earth, space, wind, and fire. The Buddha taught several meditations to enliven these inter-connections. The lemma of this law is: the inner is like the outer, and the outer is like the inner.

Examples of Buddhist principles are impermanence (all composed things are bound to decay), reincarnation (there is a continuum of life cycles), and dependent origination (we are not self-created), along with the interconnectedness of all beings and phenomena. Needless to say, we need to address all these laws and principles with more depth!

This holistic perspective embraces the view that most phenomena are rather complex, containing many causes and conditions that contribute to today's human problems. On the other hand, we experience that most so-called "modern" solutions may sometimes offer rather fragmented or compartmentalized recommendations for action, focusing only on a handful of specific aspects without considering the broader context. Here, the practice of equanimity is not only relevant but indispensable.

V. *The Need for Long-Term Sustainability:* There is a big question as to whether we are more bound to short-term solutions than longer-term and sustainable ones. Many of the outcomes of the last industrial revolution offered short-term solutions to poverty, social unrest, and economic instability. But, as we witness today, such paradigm of industrial growth and development has created many forms of decay in our societies: pollution, biodiversity depletion, global warming, and much more. Nobody in the 19th century paid attention to these long-term problems.

There must be an effort to evaluate the medium and long-term impacts of the selected Buddhist and non-Buddhist solutions. The Buddha refers to this issue in several sutras dealing with wealth creation and distribution. He states that if the system were to work in the long term, there must be a balance between the creation of material wealth and the promotion of individual and collective ethical behavior, which will end up in a more solid social equilibrium and environmental equanimity. The ethics proposed will counterbalance the risks of moving away from the right action as a result of too much wealth (greed, excessive accumulation, concentration in a few hands).

In addition, some believe that meditation is a sufficient condition for a sustainable solution. While meditation does contribute significantly to Buddhist sustainable solutions, more is needed; i.e., one must embrace Meditation Plus: it is that meditation which is fully immersed with the practice of the whole Buddhist Dharma. It is essential to add that nature plays a fundamental role in Buddhist solutions—it is not only about human wellbeing but the wellbeing of all sentient beings and nature. It is here that the common notion of environmental and social sustainability is addressed in detail.

This emphasis demands an entirely different paradigm from the one practiced today, within which our Earth is a "thing" and not a "living being." The solutions we are looking for must aim at creating long-term, lasting benefits for individuals and society as a whole.

Many people experience modern solutions as mere quick fixes that do not necessarily lead to sustainable outcomes.

VI. *The Importance of the Four Noble Truths:* The Four Noble Truths are considered the foundational teachings of Buddhism. They outline the nature of suffering (dukkha), the causes of suffering (samudaya), the cessation of suffering (nirodha), and the path to the cessation of suffering (magga).

Solutions must not increase suffering for any form of life.

Whether a solution causes suffering or not has not been a criterion for selection and decision-making today. Thus, it has become mandatory that any solution proposed must address all or any of these. It is relevant for people to know whether policymakers are because some solutions may be contributing to more suffering.

While these truths are sought to understand the nature of human existence and the root causes of suffering, they also define at least two paths for alternative solutions: one, the elimination of the causes and conditions of suffering; and two, the elimination of suffering via the practices of virtues. These are truly essential to the evaluation of any solution proposed to resolve world problems.

VII. *Other Considerations:* From the Buddha's First Discourse until his passing away, many key teachings are extremely useful in addressing most aspects of modern human reality, more than two thousand years later. These teachings form the basis of a Social Doctrine, which must become central to the construction of humanity's new future. Above, we briefly addressed the importance of "The Four Noble Truths". We may have a concise outline of several aspects of relevant social teachings:

THE NOBLE EIGHTFOLD PATH:

Perhaps one of the most fundamental teachings to shape and develop public policymaking worldwide. It includes Right Vision and Understanding, Right Intent or Resolve, Right Speech and Language, Right Action,

Right Livelihood and Behavior, Right Effort, Right Mindfulness, and Right Concentration and Meditation. Today, we face a great crisis of vision and understanding. It is not all about the right action. This crisis stems from the fact that we are living in a planetary society, while most decision-makers are still behaving as if we all are separate entities, separate nations, and the like. This is not about attaining a level of material satisfaction, as most people describe humanity's problems. The Buddha is extremely clear about how one understands and attains the Right Vision. It is evident that if we are on the path defined by the wrong vision, it would be impossible to shift and turn into a wholesome path for humanity. All is being said, even though all eight dimensions are intimately interrelated. However, when there is no agreement on what the Right Vision should be, most solutions will deepen rather than resolve the problems at hand.

THE FIVE PRECEPTS:

These precepts form the basis of individual and social ethical guidelines, in the sense that they focus on the relationships between us and other human beings, sentient beings, and nature. Thus, they contain guidelines about individual and collective behavior, about inner and outer issues and concerns, about material and spiritual challenges, and about intertemporal choices we make, which will affect ourselves and others. These Five Precepts are: to refrain from taking any form and manifestation of life—not to kill (emphasis on sentient beings like animals); to refrain from taking what is not given to us—not to steal (emphasis also on what is happening at the planetary level); to refrain from the misuse of our senses (emphasis on sensual pleasures); to refrain from wrong speech and language (emphasis on lies, untruth, verbal violence); and to refrain from consuming toxic substances (emphasis on clouding the mind through alcohol, drugs, bad thoughts).

THE MIDDLE WAY:

This is perhaps the most important concept for public policymaking: "the other path," not the average path. The Middle Way calls for new solutions that are not for self-gratification or self-mortification—i.e., avoid choosing solutions that will position us on one extreme of reality. As the Buddha taught in his First Discourse, the only road to the Middle Way is the practice of 'The Noble Eightfold Path', which provides the foundation for investment, policy, and program identification, appraisal, implementation, and evaluation—all essential for the choice of wholesome solutions. This also applies to issues related to corporate management.

THE SIX PARAMITAS:

Also called transcendent perfections, which include generosity, ethical conduct, patience, diligence, meditation, and wisdom. A group of virtues, values, or attributes that should be embodied in every Buddhist solution. It is important to underscore the importance of ethical conduct when most human activities today are carried out within an ethical vacuum. It is the absence of ethics that has accelerated the downfall of the present social doctrine in both the East and the West.

THE FOUR IMMENSURABLES *(BRAHMA VIHĀRAS):*

Loving-kindness, compassion, sympathetic joy, and equanimity. The absence of equanimity implies being away from the truth and of reality as it really is, injustice and human rights violations, ecological destruction, and much more.

These are transcendental building blocks of a Buddhist Social Doctrine. We call for total coherence among spiritual laws, spiritual principles, and spiritual instruments. Perhaps this is the most complex challenge we are facing now as well as in the future.

One has to remember the many times the Buddha spoke to businesspeople. The Buddha was fully aware of the possible applications of the principles to corporate management.

THE PRACTICES

Are there other ingredients in Buddhist decision-making? Buddhist decision-making is often guided by principles and practices that align with the core teachings of the Buddha. When making decisions, the following ingredients or factors are considered:

☐ **MINDFULNESS.** Practicing mindfulness allows individuals to be fully present and aware of their thoughts, emotions, and intentions. By cultivating mindfulness, countries can make decisions with clarity and insight, free from distractions and biases.

☐ **COMPASSION.** Compassion is a central value in Buddhism, and it plays a significant role in decision-making. The Buddha saw the need to establish a policy framework where the well-being of all forms and manifestations of life is considered, with decisions that promote kindness, empathy, and non-violence.

☐ **WISDOM.** Societies must go beyond simple knowledge and establish themselves on the throne of wisdom, which is cultivated through study, reflection, and meditation. Decision-making guided by wisdom means having a deep understanding of vital Buddhist principles, including impermanence, interconnectedness, and the nature of suffering.

☐ **ETHICAL CONSIDERATIONS.** It is vital to become responsible for the consequences of our actions—both over space and time. In an interdependent world, this is a crucial understanding for finding the most wholesome solutions to humanity's problems. This is why Buddhism insists on emphasizing the importance of ethical choices, behavior, and moral values. These form the foundation of solutions and practices at both individual and collective levels. Consider, for example, the power of social equanimity.

☐ **NON-ATTACHMENT.** Traditional solutions seldom consider the importance of non-attachment. Thus, decision-making must be approached with an open mind and a willingness to let go of personal biases and desires. Non-attachment allows decisions and choices to be based on wisdom and compassion rather than selfish motivations.

☐ **RIGHT INTENT.** In the Noble Eightfold Path, right intention is one of the factors that guide ethical conduct. Buddhist solutions must always be free of greed, hatred, and delusion, and instead be rooted in kindness, compassion, and wisdom.

☐ **EQUANIMITY.** Equanimity is the ability to remain balanced and composed in the face of changing circumstances and outcomes. Buddhist solutions must create the spaces and opportunities to cultivate the virtue of equanimity and provide the seed for a sense of calmness and inner peace, independently of the outcome.

OTHER CONSIDERATIONS

The Human Being is Only One Element of the Whole Natural System. This is truly a hallmark of Buddhism, which considers all expressions of life, sentient beings, and nature included. Thus, the analysis and evaluation of possible solutions must be carried out on how they affect all expressions of life and not only human beings. This represents a tremendous departure from the present system of decision-making. We are co-inhabitants of this planet within a system of interdependent mutuality. All expressions of life are inseparable.

This point is expanded in the chapter addressing the teachings about social policy. It is not a human-centered policy.

The Importance of Liberation as a Fruit of Action. What we know at this point is that most proposed solutions keep us further away from liberation and freedom—freedom from all sorts of material, emotional, and thought-related attachments, in a society where "more is better." The Buddha is clear on the issue of wealth accumulation and its ethical and happiness-related risks. VIMUTI is essential in deciding solutions for the individual as well as society as a whole. Inner freedom and social freedom are both relevant. Material development must be balanced by inner human development. There must be a total balance among all components of a solution; e.g., peace, happiness, and nature preservation. Peace refers to the principal ingredient of living together. Happiness refers to the quality-enhancing factor of our right livelihood. And nature preservation refers to the space, the terrain, within which our spiritual path is defined and manifested daily. The final aim is to embrace and nurture our highest expression of consciousness.

The Absence of a Wrong View. To arrive at the Right Vision, the Buddha recommends becoming the master of the wrong view and, by correcting the wrong aspects, one will find and embrace the Right Vision of life. That is to say, "to know reality as it really is." It is important to consider the fact that the Right Vision is between the Right Meditation (Samadhi) and the Right Intent, in addition to being influenced by all the ingredients of the Noble Eightfold Path.

The Two Paths of the Four Noble Truths. The Buddha offers two important solutions to address Dukka: the progressive elimination of the causes and conditions, and the effective practice of virtues and implementation of merits. This is rather unique and made explicit within Buddhist solutions. It is not like the majority of existing solutions, which address only the symptoms, and thus, the problems persist, and the outcomes of those solutions are short-lived.

The Noble Eightfold Path as a Diagnostic Method. There are many applications of the Noble Eightfold Path. One of them is as a diagnostic tool to identify more precisely the possible Buddhist solutions in a given set of circumstances. It could also be applied to families, communities, countries, and the world at large. It has proven very effective. Today, there is a tremendous lack of Right Vision! The framework has also been used in the corporate world and has served as a basis for designing and developing business models and corporate strategies.

The New Energy Which Will Get Rid of the Old One. The world needs new energies to choose and implement new solutions. The old energies are deficient and reflect a tremendously unhealthy situation. The question here is how to get rid of the old energies that are having a negative influence on our communities and the planet. One such solution is the creation of a new energy that will, in essence, "eat" the old energy. Thus, the energy of compassion will get rid of the energy of anger and greed. This suggestion has been an extremely effective paradigm of healing.

There are hundreds of sources of human and sentient beings' suffering. Some are individually based, while others are collective in nature. There is a tremendous preoccupation with the collective suffering that affects a great deal of the population. This is something that needs to be addressed with new solutions; Buddhist solutions, including group meditation. Thus, economics, politics, and institutional development must not lead to suffering of any sort; then, it is important to select instruments and solutions that do not expand the suffering we are experiencing today, individual and collective suffering.

The teachings of Buddha Shakyamuni are filled with possible solutions that enable us to follow the Middle Way. In particular, to avoid living on the extremes (e.g., transitory happiness and flagellation). But it is essential to realize that the Middle Way is not "the average" of any two extremes. It goes far beyond those extremes, in any form or fashion. This understanding—that the Middle Way is a totally different spiritual path—is extremely important when addressing, for example, the notion of the Right Livelihood. As citizens of this planet, we need to find the proper livelihood while assuming all our rights and responsibilities over space and time. The same applies to the Right Speech, Action, Effort, and Mindfulness.

Establish New Notions of Human Wellbeing.

The traditional notions of human well-being are extremely materialistic in nature. The indicators have more to do with material possessions than anything else. These forms of measuring welfare and well-being are incomplete or erroneous most of the time. Buddhist solutions have to go much further than that and include human and institutional aspects, which in the end describe a better human reality in different societies. In Buddhism, one is to account for both material and spiritual well-being and include the well-being of human beings, sentient beings, and nature.

The Meditation Factor and the Relevance of Inner Solutions.

Meditation is an essential ingredient of all possible Buddhist solutions. This ensures that we are choosing the most enlightened and highest consciousness solutions of all. This is so despite the fact that meditation can also be a very concrete and specific solution to many of the problems facing humanity. Meditation is the most important "enhancement factor" for all possible solutions. It is also a factor that ensures the maximum expression in the content and scope of solutions.

The Critical Importance of Self-Governance.

One of the most important characteristics of a Buddhist solution is to rely on individual forms of governance. This surges from a process of inner and outer empowerment. Thus, solutions that do not empower people and community structures are often not Buddhist. Buddhist solutions promote interdependence rather than dependence, be it of an economic, political, or social nature. These solutions empower rather than disempower the participation of all beings in development and transformation.

Solutions That Lead to Attaining the Full Potential of the Mind.

It is the mind—the instrument and vehicle of individual and societal change. If one is to choose the right solutions, these must reflect the state of the mind as well as influence the positive change of the mind. Solutions cannot remain outside the domain of the mind. Solutions are the mirror image of the clarity and purity of the mind. Thus, solutions must always enhance the clarity and purity of the mind.

In Buddhist solutions, the causes and conditions are equally important as the actual impacts of those solutions. Many actions are evaluated by the deeds and the impacts those deeds have and influence everyone, everywhere. This is extremely important in solutions that are charged with negative external effects, either on a new human being, sentient being, or nature. Given the intensely interdependent character of life today, caring about causes and impacts simultaneously has become a relevant imperative. Today, most solutions care only about addressing symptoms and not impacts over space and time.

Establish a Path of Moderation and Frugality:

More is Not Better. Most often than not, in today's world, to possess more is better, to buy more is better, to produce more is better, and the like. There are no incentives to moderation or to live a frugal life. In this realm, every desire has become a need to be satisfied, no matter what. Thus, we buy clothing not only to satisfy our basic needs but also because it is in fashion. The amount of waste this type of solution generates is destroying our planet and the possibilities to attain a harmonious livelihood for the benefit of all forms and manifestations of life.

The Three Supremacies:

Oneself, World, and Dharma. Every time one chooses any given solution, this has to be impregnated with three supreme ingredients of influential factors: individual transformation and not retrogression, world or societal net improvements and not recession, and Buddhist teachings and not just any sort of knowledge or opinion. In essence, these are the three criteria that establish a true Buddhist solution: whether or not it embodies human transformation and social transformation based on the power of Dharma.

The Meaning of Success:

In most societies, notions of success are defined by possession, accumulation, hoarding, having more, ego power generated, material supremacy, etc. Often, the solutions proposed today create more suffering, fear, instability, short-lived happiness, and greed. Thus, the so-called success is gained at the expense of many precious aspects of our lives. This needs to change. Therefore, the true meaning of success must be highly correlated with positive inner transformation, individual and social empowerment, and accumulated wisdom that emerges from the solutions proposed. In selecting new solutions, we must take into consideration both the self and the other, simultaneously. Thus, for example, it is not just a matter of self-realization of passion but, at the same time, committing ourselves to the construction of a compassionate society. However, this must be a wise form of construction. Supreme wisdom must become essential in all cases. Also, it is important to identify solutions related to several abstentions.

The Value of The Right Action.

There are many ways to define the Right Action, but one useful definition in the context of Buddhist solutions is: "the right action is that which does not negatively affect others and nature." This is essential in defining Buddhist solutions. Non-Buddhist solutions often do not account for the negative external effects of their embodied actions. Examples of negative actions on others include pollution of water and air, the generation of addiction, the expansion of greed, and more desires.

Solutions That Generate Desirable and Favorable Conditions.

It is imperative to find solutions that (i) do not destroy existing desirable conditions of livelihood (e.g., destroying natural forests) or (ii) create favorable conditions for living and self-realization for all manifestations of life. In particular, Buddhist solutions must create good conditions for those the Buddha called "stream enterers," those prepared to commit to the full practice of the Dharma. Today, there are too many distractions, vices, and aspects of life people cling to, thus eliminating the possibility of conditions for stream enterers. Some argue for less work and more productive leisure. Though it may sound strange, many solutions end up creating more slavery and social structures that do not lead to liberation. This is what we call a "veiled caste system" of privileged people in our societies who are served in a pyramidal way, well described in the Sutras of the Buddha. Remember that the Buddha was a tremendous social reformer. We are now slaves to different products (drugs), different forms of twisted marketing (false advertising), and inadequate lifestyles (ecological destruction). People are "serving too many masters": economic masters, political masters, religious masters, institutional masters, corporate masters...

The Bundle of Solutions Must Bring the Union of Truth & Conduct.

Solutions must not only follow the truth (dharma), but they must also translate into Right Behavior. This includes good habits, adequate friends, and the practice of important virtues such as generosity and compassion. Furthermore, solutions must induce people to perform merits (boon) and serve everyone everywhere. Conduct or behavior lies between Right Action and Right Effort within the Noble Eightfold Path; thus, it is greatly influenced by our actions (karma) and our willingness to apply the right effort to accomplish the goals for which those solutions were designed.

Solutions That Enhance Perception, Consciousness, and Wisdom.

Evaluating the best options for selecting solutions, including Buddhist ones, demands awareness about perception (the power of understanding wholesome and unwholesome actions and decisions), our level of consciousness, and ability (skillful means) to reach high levels of sati (mindfulness) and embrace the highest levels of wisdom possible (pañña). It is imperative to select solutions that lead toward intelligent investments. The intelligence of investments is directly proportional to the space they create for the self-realization of all beings. All beings are on the path to enlightenment.

The Principles of Impermanence, Non-Dukkha, and Non-Self.

Solutions must not give the impression of permanence. This is the illusion created by most solutions in the 21st century, and unfortunately, people behave accordingly. Within this context, we are experiencing individual as well as collective suffering of all sorts. Buddhist solutions are always geared to eliminate suffering, not to multiply it. Many of today's solutions feed our ego, creating a sense of an independent self and a stage that feeds some sort of absolute existence.

Marketing is a great tool for such an ego strategy. Most non-Buddhist solutions concentrate only on their very short-term impacts (e.g., I buy an apple and satisfy that desire to buy the apple). The apple is sold, and it seems that is all that matters. However, there are many impacts resulting from any given solution (e.g., the consumption of that apple may end up causing diarrhea or a stomach infection). Thus, second and third-round effects may be very negative and concerning. A typical example is a solution via the creation of a factory to create employment; however, that factory may also pollute and create major health effects to workers as well as the population at large. There are many examples of negative long-term effects. Buddhist solutions are not of that nature.

Adopt a Spiritual Practice that is Connected to Society.

Most non-Buddhist solutions are designed to benefit very few people, leaving the rest of society in a perilous situation. In a global economic system that creates incentives to expand individual materialism, this phenomenon is widespread. There are incentives and policies to accumulate, hoard, and possess as much as possible in a few hands. The teachings of the Buddha on creation, sharing, and spending material wealth are a good illustration of a good Buddhist solution in this case. One must go much further than purely individual benefits. In a planet with more than 10 billion people, this is a very relevant issue to consider.

The Principle of Personal and Social Responsibility.

In a world characterized by total interdependence, solutions must consider the notions of rights and shared responsibilities. The common good is now tremendously important, and it is the responsibility of everyone to take care of it. Buddhist solutions create awareness of these commonly held goods for the benefit of all beings. These common goods include climate, ozone layer, glaciers, oceans, rivers, culture, values, security, justice, migration, and health, among others. The Buddha was very explicit in saying that it is not only about individual responsibility but also about social responsibility. We do not live in uniform societies. Also, we cannot make societies uniform. Each person carries their own karma: karmic path and karmic debts. This is really what makes us different, and no other form of modern identity. Buddhist solutions respect the constancy of human nature and thus can benefit all beings, independently of their karmic reality at present. This is not the case with non-Buddhist solutions. We see this in existing education systems, mostly oriented to external knowledge and not inner wisdom. It is the path to inner wisdom that enables all of us to benefit from spiritual development, no matter who we are and where we have been born.

The Creation of Virtuous Societies.

It seems that the solutions we are applying to today's issues and challenges are creating communities that are losing their inner virtues. They are conforming to a culture in fashion and not to their fundamental culture and values. Globalization replaces individual cultures with some sort of global culture: a new age. Buddhist solutions must strengthen the bounty of cultures and values rather than replace them with a uniform code that diminishes the true identity and sense of belonging everywhere. It is imperative to select solutions that will lead towards higher virtues, higher minds, and higher wisdom.

The Complementarity of Dhamma and Vinaya.

Buddhist solutions come from Buddha's teachings, as stated in many texts, including the Sutras and the Vinaya (the rules of engagement, the administration of justice, and application of justiciability, as regards behavior in monastic communities and elsewhere). Buddhist solutions bring about a natural and organic balance and application of the Dhamma as expressed in the Sutras and the Vinaya. Today, we need a "Planetary Vinaya." It is inexistent!

To Establish a Clear Sense of Purpose.

All Buddhist solutions must have a clear purpose of eliminating suffering and bringing all beings to full enlightenment. The word "sense" here refers to solutions that have emerged from the right process of discernment so that we engage in the right path of wholesome actions and behaviors. It is purposeless to embrace solutions that will lead to the wrong path of unwholesome human reality (drugs, prostitution, weaponry, war, conflict, greed, ego, etc.). We must always ask about purpose. A solution without a clear purpose and intent is like a dry leaf flying at the mercy of today's winds—without direction.

Examples of
Social Teachings
of The Buddha

Chapter 5:

THE CONDITIONS OF WELFARE OF A NATION

(THE MAHAPARANIRBANA SUTTA)

"The more we take the welfare of others to hear and work for their benefit, The more benefit we derive for ourselves"

Dalai Lama

The social teachings of the Buddha are infinite in numbers and, thus, it is impossible to present them in one book. A selected number of these teachings will be outlined here, with the view to illustrate the many foundations and thematic richness of Buddhism. They show a Buddha deeply engaged in the importance of properly governing our materiality.

The Sutra begins in a very special way: a conflict between the king of Maghada and the population of the Vajjis. The king promises to annihilate them by all means possible. In the teachings of *THE MA-HAPARANIRBANA SUTRA*, the Buddha uses as a point of departure a situation depicting some important conflict between two kingdoms; a warlike situation. It is not random that a given "conflict" is being used as the vehicle of teaching (the skillful means). Very similar to the Bhagavad Gita: which concentrates on the teaching of Karma Yoga and the nature of transcendental consciousness.

In this particular text, the essential element of the teaching is to gain an understanding of the need we have to address and change our notion of WELL-BEING at the collective level (at a societal level), and realize, based in that notion of wellbeing, how a given society pursuing it, may truly become invincible. A notion which goes far beyond a military defense mechanism, or the use of a brute force at play. A notion of invincibility worth considering today, as we are surrounded by military conflicts all over the world.

It is very relevant to add a vital consideration, to fully understand this teaching, understanding a nation as "a mandala". Specifically, this has to do with the notion of "invincibility" and its embodied 'sacred geometry'; e.g., the distribution, location and intensity of the protection-wisdom-energy within the mandala, as the defense mechanism.

While the King of Magadha governed his mandala (nation) through strengthening the borders of the said mandala, the Buddha offers the king a very different solution: to protect a nation from powerful energies located at the center of the mandala—the basic notion of invincibility.

While the king supported a border-protection-weapons-solution, the Buddha responds with a more subtle and potent dimension of invincibility: wisdom energy. It seems important to look more closely at this particular dimension of the Sutra. This teaching is of particular benefit around nations experiencing conflicts and their possible resolutions. The teachings of this Sutra present clearly two very different paths towards everlasting peace.

This, in itself, deserves a great deal of thought, silence and meditation about these two very different ways to govern a given mandala, and avoiding conflicts with others. In this case, the mandala may be your own self.

We know that, in economics, there are many notions of 'well-being'; generally, these notions are very materialistic in nature (i.e., the possession of material wealth). Here, on the contrary, the notion of well-being is tremendously revolutionary, as we will see in a moment.

One of the most beautiful dimensions of this story is the recognition of the "(social and political) authority" of the Buddha by the King of Magadha. Thus, not only personal spiritual authority, within an individual spiritual path, but also, a significant authority within the realm of conflict resolution, as a society addressed collective, social, institutional, geographic and political conflicts. This situation shows us that the vision and presence of the Buddha was very much valued, and that his equanimity in public decision making were well known at that time. As I said before, this is the birth and development of the social dimension of Buddhism. He did not shy away from these dimensions.

The Sutra is very explicit. There is not much to guess. In particular, a key statement in the text is when King Ajatasattu says, *"Go to him, because the Buddha does not speak falsehoods."* How gravitating this is! Particularly, in contingent politics at the national and international levels. Nobody trusts politics or politicians. Something on which we must meditate deeply; i.e., the importance of "trust" in addressing collective issues. This "trust" on the Buddha shows how important the foundations of one's spirituality is in delivering strategic alternatives regarding how should we live and behave in any society. It is an explicit call for the integration of spirituality in economics, politics and business. A similar challenge to the integration of religion and science through human history. Today, there is no trust.

> **This is the birth and development of the social dimensions of Buddhism**

Everything happens in a respectful manner, and within a dialogue that contains lots of meaningful protocols. This is how the King tells his emissary, his Prime Minister: upon arrival at the place where the Buddha was, you must wish the Buddha good health, strength, tranquility, vigor and comfort. These were five important offerings. To me, this list of offerings represents a master piece on what we may wish to our beloved Masters, thanking them for their unique and indispensable presence on this Planet Earth.

Health, Strength, Tranquility, Vigor and Comfort

In this dialogue, everything becomes a true recognition of where "spiritual authority" lies and eventually manifested. Also, it shows us the role that "truth" and "trust" play as an important element of such societal authority.

After the King's conflicts and wishes, for the total annihilation of his enemies, are made known within the dialogue, the elements associated with the Buddha's responses (his advice to him) were astonishing. The Buddha answered in an indirect way, by asking Ananda a series of questions related to what he knows of the Vajjis. For me, this manner of teaching on the part of the Buddha is simply amazing: a perfect balance between the right set of questions and the right set answers to construct the concept of "invincibility of a nation".

The questions were very precise and pointed, and the final answer was categorical. Everything is transformed into enumerating The Conditions of Well-Being of a Nation, and defining how such form of well-being makes that Nation invincible and indestructible. All the questions begin like this: *"What have you heard, Ananda..."?* The Buddha knew very well what questions to ask. And, the Sutra continues with the Buddha's hypotheses. Here, the method is not only about asking the right question but also define a way to gathering information about where some social consensus should or could emerge. The Buddha, via the phrase on what Ananda has *"heard from the people"*, builds a perfect notion and feasible path towards social equanimity *(UPEKKA)*.

1. 'If the Vajjis meet periodically, and if the meetings are well attended.'

In the language of this millennium, the Buddha is asking about having an assembly as a form of democracy—i.e., a participatory and deliberative forms of democracy. The teaching shows the relationship this assembly has as a source of well-being with an institutional structure to reach citizens' consensus. Extraordinarily relevant in the 21st century, where we are experiencing the greatest expressions of "citizenry". Here, the Buddha is delivering an opinion about "democratic" or "participatory institutions" within a nation and their impacts on the welfare of a society. In this case, Ananda said that in the case of the Vajjis the answer was positive. The conclusion in this case, as in other dimensions of well-being (expressed below), is that the "growth" of the Vajjis is expected, and not "their decline". This form of response pattern is repeated in all the characteristics that define the main ingredients of a nation's well-being.

2. 'If the Vajjis meet in assemblies and if upon completion of their deliberations they disperse peacefully, along with addressing issues with "agreements"?

Here, the Buddha's attention expands to what happens after an assembly, after the meetings. He assumes that they have reached consensual agreements since, otherwise, they would not be released peacefully. This is a fundamental expression of real need to govern with agreements. Ultimately, the Vajjis are a society that is capable of emerging—politically and otherwise--through agreements. In the case of the Vajjis...

3. 'If the Vajjis proceed in accordance with their ancestral constitutions, instead of using new decrees or abolishing existing ones.'

Here the Buddha calls for the recognition of ancient wisdom, and the contributions that the most important traditions could make to societal welfare. He makes a call not to forget the origin of wisdom, giving great importance to our indigenous people. It is as if the Buddha appealed to a concept of 'pure wisdom'. This is a hot topic in our societies; particularly, with the rise of indigenous nations. Not a minor issue within the Latin American countries. In the case of the Vajjis...

4. 'If the Vajjis respect, honor, consider, esteem, and venerate their elders, and think that it is worth listening to them.'

This clearly shows the need to include in the debates on well-being, the true and real well-being of our senior adults: health, continues education, social security, transportation, housing, dignified aging and much more. In the case of the Vajjis...

5. 'If the Vajjis refrain from kidnapping women and maidens of good families, and if they also refrain from arresting them.'

This message from the Buddha represents a great call to consider gender issues, whatever the notion of well-being of a nation. This is another topic of vital importance in politics, economics, social and institutional. In the case of the Vajjis...

6. **'If the Vajjis show respect to their temples and holy places, both inside and outside the cities, and do not limit the people to making their offerings, made formally for those occasions.'**

That is to say, that the notions of well-being of a nation must also integrate the acts of offerings and respect for places of prayer, meditation, contemplation, etc. The Buddha makes mention of holy places in rural areas, and not just in the cities. A very relevant distinction for our times. It is also true that this question shows the relationship between spirituality and politics, and spirituality and human rights (e.g., freedom of worship). In the case of the Vajjis...

7. **'If the Vajjis duly protect the Arahats, so that those who have not yet come to the kingdom (he means the higher kingdoms) can do so, and those who have already come can live there in peace.'**

Concern for people who have those higher degrees of consciousness. If the welfare of these beings is low, the Buddha suggests that the whole society is going to suffer. That is to say his notion of well-being demands the existence of interdependence in its maximum expression. This is the well-being that arises from our inner state of being at a collective level. That is, our societies must have the capacity to accumulate wisdom and to absorb/embrace the attributes and benefits of people who have the highest states of consciousness. In short, the protection of the most enlightened beings and the protection of nature, so that they can reincarnate on Earth again. In the case of the Vajjis...

The conclusion is that the King can never bring down the Vajjis, because they meet the 7 conditions for the well-being of a nation. Time and time again, the Buddha states that: "its growth is expected, not its decline." The Buddha's final conclusion is categorical: "Indeed, the King of Magadha, Ajatasattu, cannot harm the Vajjis in battle, except through treachery or discord."

The Buddha does not rank these attributes. Therefore, he appeals to the criteria of the authorities of Magadha, making a call and a reflection, again, to the crucial importance of SELF-GOVERNANCE. This is not the first time the Buddha has expressed this (e.g., see also "The Sutra of the Lichavis").

The following is stated at the end of the Sutra:

"And the Blessed One addressed the brahman Vassakara in these words:

"Once, brahman, I dwelt at Vesali, at the Sarandada shrine, and there it was that I taught the Vajjis these seven conditions leading to (a nation's) welfare. So long, brahman, as these endure among the Vajjis, and the Vajjis are known for it, their growth is to be expected, not their decline."

"Thereupon the brahman Vassakara spoke thus to the Blessed One:

"If the Vajjis, Venerable Gotama, were endowed with only one or another of these conditions leading to welfare, their growth would have to be expected, not their decline. What then of all the seven? No harm, indeed, can be done to the Vajjis in battle by Magadha's king, Ajatasattu, except through treachery or discord. Well, then, Venerable Gotama, we will take our leave, for we have much to perform, much work to do."

"Do as now seems fit to you, brahman."

And the brahman Vassakara, the chief minister of Magadha, approving of the Blessed One's words and delighted by them, rose from his seat and departed."

Chapter 6:

THE PRINCIPLES OF GOVERNANCE FOR THE KING

(DASA RAJA DHAMMA)

"Violence is the last resort of the incompetent"

Isaac Asimov

The principal foundations of Buddhism rest on **"The Three Jewels"**: **The Buddha, the Dharma and the Sangha.** Social Buddhism rests on our understanding of the Sangha, based on Buddha's teachings (coming from the Buddha and the Dharma). The first lessons about the Sangha came directly from the Buddha as he was establishing the foundations of his Monastic Society. Then, many lessons and treaties came from his direct disciples like Ananda and Sariputha, and the great Buddhist sages, who "wrote manuscripts" (recite) during the first few centuries after the Buddha passed away.

Notions of governance were refined and put forth at the disposal of leaders far beyond those monastic societies (like the Lam Rim). One great example of a person who practiced Buddhism within the realm of politics, was King Ashoka. A very virtuous king who applied many of the Buddhist principles of governance as taught by the Buddha.

The above is really fundamental to account for, as these Buddhist principles were passed on to be applied into the everyday life of normal citizens all around the world.

Today, in our Western modern civilization there are plenty of books addressing the need for new forms of "leadership"; all these books trying to distill the attributes of a 'great' leader.

> **Notions of governance were refined and put forth at the disposal of leaders far beyond those monastic societies**

With Professor Marco Tavanti, we wrote a book entitled: **"Conscious Sustainability Leadership"**. This is a book that focuses on the self-realized leader, the spiritual leader, the transcending leader... The leader that is able to see and go far beyond the immediate. Equally, today, there are hundreds of books on the theme of Governance, on self-governance, and on how to govern a given community, a country, or even the planet. But, there are very few books on the spiritual attributes and dimensions of governance; i.e., "Conscious Governance".

During the time of the Buddha, there were many small kingdoms. Buddha Shakyamuni met with many of those kings, and taught them the supreme values of governing a country and developing the right type of politics and economics (see, for example, The Kuttadanta Sutta, among several other sutras).

One of these great teachings was known as: *DASA RAJA DHAMMA;* "The Ten Royal Virtues". This book shares the essence as grouped by Danister I. Fernando, *"Dasa-Raja-Dhamma:* The 'Ten Royal Virtues'", posted on April 23rd, 2017. It is said that the original text was not a sutra per se, but a teaching compiled after the passing away of the Buddha.

Dana: Liberality, Generosity or Charity. The giving away of alms to the needy. It is the duty of the king (government) to look after the welfare of his needy subjects. The ideal ruler should give away wealth and property wisely without giving in-to craving and attachment. In other words, he should not try to be rich making use of his position.

Sila: Morality – A High Moral Character. He must observe at least the Five Precept (i.e., no killing, no stealing, no sexual misconduct, no lying, no intoxicants), and conduct himself both in private and in public life as to be a shining example to his subjects. This virtue is very important, because, if the ruler adheres to it, strictly, then bribery and corruption, violence and indiscipline would be automatically wiped out in the country.

Pariccaga: Comfort. Making sacrifices if they are for the good of the people – personal name and fame; even the life if need be. By the grant of gifts, the ruler spurs the subjects on to more efficient and more loyal service.

Ajjava: Honesty and Integrity. He must be absolutely straightforward and must never take recourse to any crooked or doubtful means to achieve his ends. He must be free from fear or favor in the discharge of his duties. (A stanza from *'Sigalovada Sutta, Digha-Nikaya).*

Maddava: Kindness or Gentleness. A ruler's uprightness may sometimes require firmness. But this should be tempered with kindness and gentleness. In other words, a ruler should not be over harsh or cruel.

Tapa: Restraint of Senses and Austerity in Habits. Shunning indulgence in sensual pleasures, an ideal monarch keeps his five senses under control. Some rulers may, using their position, flout moral conduct – this is not becoming of a good monarch.

Akkodha: Non-Hatred. The ruler should bear no grudge against anybody. Without harboring grievances, he must act with forbearance and love. At this instance, I am reminded of how a certain royal pupil, an heir to the throne, who had been punished by the teacher for an offence, took revenge by punishing the teacher after he become King! (Jataka Text). Political victimization is also not conducive to proper administration.

Avihimsa: Non-Violence. Not only should he refrain from harming anybody but he should also try to promote peace and prevent war, when necessary. He must practice non-violence to the highest possible extent so long as it does not interfere with the firmness expected of an ideal ruler.

Khanti: Patience and Tolerance. Without losing his temper, the ruler should be able to bear up hardships and insults. In any occasion, he should be able to conduct himself without giving in-to emotions. He should be able to receive both bouquets and brickbats in the same spirit and with equanimity.

Avirodha: Non–Opposition and Non–Enmity. The ruler should not oppose the will of the people. He must cultivate the spirit of amity among his subjects. In other words, he should rule in harmony with his people.

These principles must also serve as a check list in many situations having to do with management in both the private and public sector. Human resources development department within the corporate world must take the abovementioned attributes into account when promoting people to the positions of leadership. Management and managers are not only about knowledge. It goes far beyond that. Today, we must make a call to humanize institutions everywhere, and those attributes are the scaffold to do so.

Finally, these royal virtues are a blueprint to reconcile spirituality with business and economics; now indispensable to the humanization of work, leisure, rights, responsibilities, commitment, justice, etc. There has been lots of attention to productivity and competitiveness, in a paradigm that has atomized most of human activities. Now is the time to put a face and to create a path to the self-realizations of those virtues.

Chapter 7:

WEALTH and THE BUDDHA I

(THE VYAGGHAPAJJA SUTTA)

"Few things are necessary to make a wise man happy while no amount of material wealth would satisfy a fool." "I am not a fool."

Og Mandino

Many times, the Buddha addressed important issues surrounding economic wealth (e.g., material wealth). In particular, he addressed the importance of (i) "creating wealth", (ii) "reproducing wealth", (iii) "protecting wealth", (iv) "distributing wealth" and (v) "spending wealth". All of them essential to the nature and scope of economics, finance and business. For the Buddha, the challenge was not only to create wealth, a theme embedded in our present reality. Also, wealth had to be reproduced, expanded, for the benefit of all human beings, sentient beings and nature. The expansion was not only for the benefit of the one person who created such a material wealth (hoarding, retaining, self-accumulating).

It is important to note that the Buddha saw also a fundamental and indispensable obligation to protect the wealth which has been created, and not just let that wealth to decay and disappear.

With regard to the decaying of wealth, today, we are witnesses how our 'natural wealth' (environment, ecology) decays and disappears at an alarming rate (loss of biodiversity, water and air pollution, global warming, natural forest depletion). A very serious problem, as we are irreversibly losing our natural capital.

THE VYAGGHAPAJJA SUTTA (i.e., we use here the translation from Pali by Narada Thera) is one of the sutras which presents us with some essential economics teachings. This sutra shares one out of many typical dialogues between the Buddha and a person within the corporate world—e.g., the world of business. With a very positive view and understanding about 'material wealth', the Buddha advices on how to increase and sustain wealth and avoid its loss.

The teachings are very clear with regard to the sort of inner impacts that wealth and more accumulated wealth may have onto us. More wealth may create more attachment-led desires towards it, more powerful craving to possess more and more, more strategic efforts to establishing a "power-strong-hole", etc.

Thus, the Buddha repeats many times that as there are benefits from material wealth, there are also lots of "karmic costs" associated to the process of wealth creation. He teaches us that attachment, craving, etc. are the main sources of conflicts, either within the life of an individual or the life of a society as a whole; something extremely present in our societies today.

This leads to another crucial teaching of the Buddha: the fundamental importance and urgent necessity to balancing "material wealth" with "spiritual wealth". He is very explicit on how to reach such a balance: confidence, virtue, liberality and wisdom. These will enable corporate owners and managers to have a better understanding with regard to their obligations with the rest of society.

In the teachings' enumeration of the conditions, the Buddha talks about conditions for both wealth (material) and happiness (spiritual or the ethics in the process and its impacts). This two-dimensional approach marks the difference in relation to other ways to analyze wealth and the process of wealth creation!

Ethics is very important to be considered. In the Sutra we are citing here, he refers to both: individual and social happiness (ethics).

At the core of this teaching, the Buddha recognizes at least four conditions to take into account in wealth creation: (i) the persistent effort in whatever activity one is in and simultaneously develop the power of discernment (like the Right Effort); (ii) the self-realization of watchfulness (vigilance), where wealth is acquired by the right means and do not let it be stolen, damage by fire or floods or ill-disposed heirs removed (like the Right Mindfulness—be present all the time and avoid wealth destruction); (iii) the good friendship, which is cultivated by faith (saddha), virtue (sila) charity (caga) and wisdom (panna) (like the Right Behavior); and (iv) the need for a balanced livelihood, which leads to a balanced life, not being extravagant nor miserly... (it is like the nature and scope of The Right Livelihood).

Then the teachings move to the main sources of wealth destruction: immorality, drunkenness, gambling, and friendship, companionship and intimacy with evil-doers. Something to think about and meditate.

The sutra ends with teachings about how to increase (expansion) one's wealth: abstinence from immorality, abstinence from drunkenness, non-indulgence in gambling, and friendship, companionship and intimacy with the good.

> **The Buddha talks about conditions for both wealth and happiness**

The above is as important today as it was during the time of Buddha Shakyamuni.

Chapter 8:

WEALTH and THE BUDDHA II

(THE DIGHAJANU SUTTA, THE KAAMABHOGII SUTTA, THE ANANYA SUTTA, THE PATTAKAMMA SUTTA, THE VYAGGHAPAJJA SUTTA, THE VADDHA SUTTA, THE SIGALOVADA SUTTA, THE ADIYA SUTTA)

"Let's be cautious about relying so much on material things that we have no energy left for the spiritual aspects of our lives."

James A. Forbes

Based on the teaching of several sutras, this section puts together a series of thoughts about the real essence of what we may tentatively name: 'Transformational Economics'. This considers both, the inner and outer transformations.

Most of the material brought here comes from a key-note lecture in honor of The Great Mahasiddha Lama Gangchen Tulku Rimpoche; a lecture that was never delivered. It was to be delivered at the Borobudur Temple in Yogyakarta, Indonesia, a couple of years ago. The title of the presentation was to be: "The Buddhist Mandala of Transformational Economics" (Dzambling Cho Tab Khen). Herewith another set of examples in which the Buddha addresses socially relevant issues.

In *THE DIGHAJANU SUTTA*, the Buddha speaks clearly about how to expand your wealth as well as how to avoid losing it. The essence of this sutra is that material wealth alone will not make a human being happy or a society a balance one.

The Buddha also added a link between creation of wealth and human behavior, and he warns us that more materiality creates more desires. These desires translate in more material wealth and ego-power, greed and craving. The Buddha offers an alternative which, in essence, it is an instrument to the spiritual opening the mandala of economics. He states that consciousness has to rise in order to avoid those negative situations, via the practice of trust, confidence, virtue, liberality and wisdom (like in *THE VYAGGHAPAJJA SUTTA*). These attributes will create the space for a higher sense of values.

In addition, the Buddha also established the individual and the collective responsibilities in economics. These are not only individual responsibilities. The gaining of individual material welfare should not overshadow the concern for the society as a whole (a question about who benefits from wealth). It is the combination of the spiritual and the material notions of welfare that will result in an ideal society.

In *THE KAAMABHOGII SUTTA*, the Buddha talks to a Banker, named Anaathapindika, and explained him the many attitudes that people may have as regards wealth. These different attitudes form a model of economic behavior.

One of the key aspects of this Sutra is the sharing of wealth. This is a key issue with millions of ramifications. Not easy to address but we all know how concentrated wealth is in the world today, and how economics plays a fundamental role in that concentration. As a matter of fact, globalization has been a tremendous accelerator in concentrating wealth in just a few hands. This means control and the accumulation of political power in a few hands. In laymen's terms, the sutra speaks out about the negative spiritual consequences that inequality has.

> **One of the key aspects of the Sutra is the sharing of wealth**

When speaking to Anathapindika, the buddha established four kinds of happiness: (i) the happiness that emanates from ownership, i.e., a lawful way to earn your wealth; (ii) the happiness that emanates from wealth, i.e., a proper way to enjoy the wealth you earned lawfully; (iii) the happiness that emanates from not having debts (debtlessness), i.e., do not owe to anyone; and (iv) the happiness that emanates from not being blamed (blamelessness) i.e., a form of life which is blessed by good deeds (right actions, boon) of the body, mind and speech. (THE ANANYA SUTTA). In some way, the first three are related with what you have created and the last one contains the corresponding positive consequences.

In sum, material wealth represents also a foundation for both material and spiritual development.

All of the above is repeated in *THE PATTAKAMMA SUTTA*. There, the Buddha states four fundamental "wishes":

1. **Wealth must come from lawful means;**
2. **Good reputation in society;**
3. **Live a long and healthy life; and**
4. **Happiness after death.**

In *THE VADDHA SUTTA* the Buddha specifically speaks about growth, including economic growth. Naturally, he does it in the language and with the examples pertaining to a rural based society, more than 2500 years ago. The essential message is that one cannot grow a material dimension only, like with more grain, more buildings, more animals, more corporate power, more workers, etc.

The Buddha explicitly states that we need to grow also in terms of faith, virtue, love, generosity, and wisdom. We need to explore much more the connection between these two groups of attributes: material and spiritual. But, we clearly know and are experiencing what happens when economics is grown without wisdom. This is the difference between focusing on growth and on human and sentient beings' evolution. Economics has to focus on both.

It is clear that the Buddha gave lots of importance to economics and to establishing the real importance of material wealth. Thus, the Buddha made many people aware of the relationship between poverty and spirituality. A poor person struggles against poverty, and the mind is loaded with that. The worrying about the prospects that poverty brings into life, distorts the spiritual path. It also overshadows some notion of moral responsibility of the human collective. This does not mean living without an awareness of our collective interdependence. In *THE DHAMMAPADA*, verse 203, the Buddha states: *"hunger is the most severe illness"*.

THE SIGALOVADA SUTTA states that a master should look after servants and employees (THE COLLECTIVE) by:

(**1**) "by assigning them work according to their ability,

(**2**) "by supplying them with food and with wages,

(**3**) "by tending them in sickness,

(**4**) "by sharing with them any delicacies,

(**5**) "by granting them leave at times" (Digha Nikaya 31).

Early Buddhist texts see success in work related activities as aided by one's spiritual and moral qualities.

In *THE ADIYA SUTTA* the Buddha also outlined several ways in which people could put their 'righteously gained' (gained through lawful means) wealth to use:

'Providing 'pleasure & satisfaction' to themselves, their mother & father, their children, spouse, slaves, servants, & assistants.
'Providing 'pleasure & satisfaction' to their friends and associates.
'Warding off calamities coming from fire, flood, kings, thieves, or hateful heirs, and keeps himself safe.
'Performs five oblations/offerings: to relatives, guests, the dead, kings, & devas.
'Giving of offerings to priests (brahmins) and contemplatives (monks)'.

The Buddha placed much emphasis on the virtue of giving and sharing, and hence the practice of donating and charity are central to buddhist economic ethics.

Even the poor are encouraged to share, because this brings about greater spiritual wealth:

> *"If beings knew, as I know, the results of giving & sharing, they would not eat without having given, nor would the stain of selfishness overcome their minds. Even if it were their last bite, their last mouthful, they would not eat without having shared, if there were someone to receive their gift."*

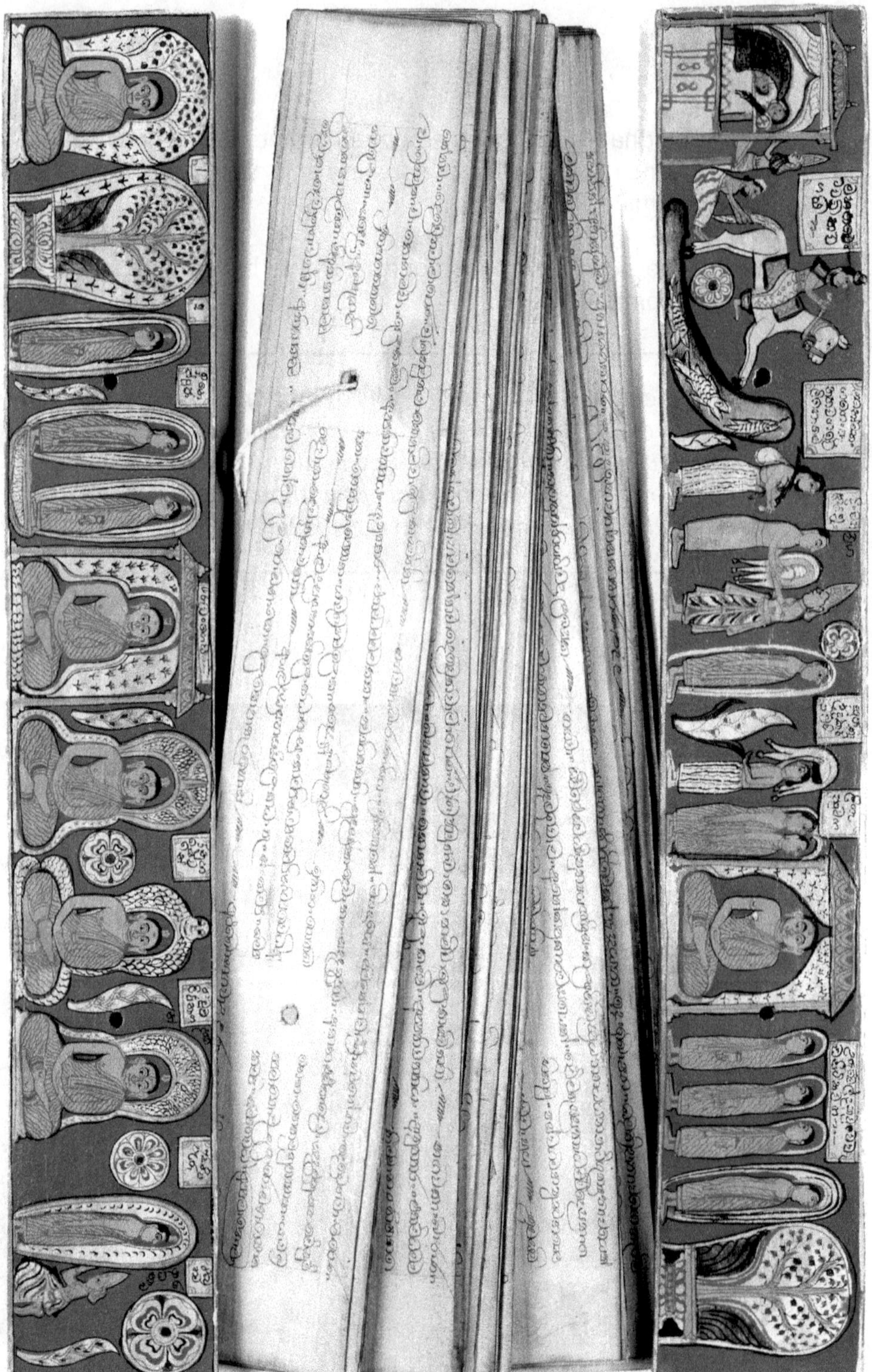

Chapter 9:

WEALTH and THE BUDDHA III

(THE SIGALOVADA SUTTA, THE ANANYA SUTTA, THE PATTAKAMMA SUTTA, THE APUTTAKA SUTTA)

"Not he who has much is rich, but he who gives much."

Erich Fromm

The Buddha was very explicit regarding the proper use of wealth. This is important because, many people, have the impression that Buddhism is out of the realm of hard economics and material wealth. The essence of the teaching is that materiality is an intrinsic dimension of our spiritual evolution. In fact, with the proper understanding, material wealth may be an important vehicle to practice some important virtues, like that of generosity and interdependence. Furthermore, in some circumstances, the absence of material wealth—basic resource to have a minimum standard of living—often causes suffering.

But this is a narrow road between basic material livelihood and being obsessed and greedy. A theme the Buddha refers to in many Sutras. Greed is a very important cause in the creation of negative Karma. As stated in *THE SIGALOVADA SUTTA*, the Buddha suggested how to proportionately spend one's wealth.

Pay attention to it please:

1. Half should be spent on business, implying a serious necessity to keep creating and maintaining wealth.

2. One quarter of one's wealth is suggested to be spent on enjoyment, implying that the productivity of your leisure is extremely important in our spiritual path (e.g., silence, joy, contemplation, good friendships...).

3. And, last but not least, the last quarter must be saved. These are very important statements to be reflected upon, constantly.

The above may have important ramifications for policy debates at the macro level of a nation, as well as at the global level.

According to other sacred Buddhist scriptures, it is said that wealth should (i) bring happiness to oneself, families, friends and employees. It is interesting the mentioning of the importance of bringing happiness to the employees; (ii) protect the wealth from losses and mal management. In fact, my reading of the Buddha's teaching is that the protection of wealth is an important obligation. Once you have wealth, you are bound to protect it; (iii) give offerings to many beings that are mutually interdependent, including gods, when offerings are an important component of Buddhist spirituality; and (iv) give gifts to those who share wisdom and virtues. See THE ANANYA SUTTA for some details and more.

The debate on happiness also touches on the theme of wealth and possessions. In particular, the Buddha said that there is happiness from material ownership, consumption and freedom from debt, among others.

One of the main sources of happiness is sharing wealth. At one point the Buddha stated that if we knew the benefits from sharing we would change our habits and behaviors. Specifically, the Buddha stated: 'even if it were their last bit, their last morsel of food, they would not enjoy its use without sharing it if there was someone else to share it with.'

In *THE PATTAKAMMA SUTTA*, the Buddha teaches about the importance of basic needs and the relationship with our spiritual evolution. He states that wealth must come by lawful means. And, that worries about food, clothing and shelter move people away from reflection, transcendental awareness... This is essential in the debate about economics and human welfare. But this economics must be inserted into an ethical conduct all the time.

Once I asked why there were very few Buddhist monks in Africa? The answer was categorical: they have not satisfied their basic needs yet. Needless to say, that I am in total disagreement with such answer. This is a wrong interpretation of the Buddha's teachings. Spiritual values, and decisions based on those values are essential at every step of human evolution.

There is a very important sutra that describes the true meaning of wealth, including its distribution, among many. This is *THE APUTTA-KA SUTTA*. The recommendations of the Buddha are self-explanatory:

> *"Just as with a pond not far from a town or village,*
> *with clear water, cool water, fresh water, clean,*
> *with good fords, delightful.*
> *People would draw water from it or drink it*
> *or bathe in it or apply it to their needs.*
> *And so, that water, properly put to use,*
> *would go to a good use and not to waste.*
> *In the same way, when a person of integrity*
> *acquires lavish wealth...*
> *his wealth, properly put to use,*
> *goes to a good use and not to waste."*

"That is what the Blessed One said. Having said that, the One Well-Gone, the Teacher, said further:

"Like water in a haunted place
that, without being imbibed,
dries up: such is the wealth
acquired by a worthless person
who neither enjoys it himself nor gives.
But one enlightened & knowing,
on acquiring wealth, enjoys it & performs
his duties.
He, a bull among men, having supported his kin,
without blame goes to the land of heaven."

Chapter 10:
WEALTH and THE BUDDHA IV
(THE ADIYA SUTTA)

"Wealth is but dung, useful only when spread about."

Chinese Proverb

The Buddha also focused on the use of wealth and its benefits. This is a very important element as, in my view, how do we spend our wealth is more important than the level of wealth.

This is a very important issue in fiscal economics: notwithstanding the relevance of fiscal incomes and revenues, it is equally important to adequately determine how the government should spend it. Thus, it is not only an issue of individual gains and expenditures; it is also an issue of collective gains and expenditures.

The key concern of the Buddha is with the potential impacts of those expenditures. In the previous presentation, we focused on how one earns wealth. Here, how one spend that wealth. The presentation here is based on *THE ADIYA SUTTA:* Benefits to be Obtained (from Wealth) (see translation by Thanissaro Bhikkhu. 1997).

For the Buddha, there are five benefits that can be obtained from wealth:

1. To maintain one's right pleasures and satisfaction. This includes the family, children, wife, servants...

2. To provide pleasure and satisfaction to the friends and associates (co-workers).

3. Wards off calamities from fire, flood, guests, death, kings, thiefs, and keep himself safe.

4. Offerings to relatives, guests, dead, kings and devas.

5. Offerings of supreme aim of unbinding (brahmans, contemplatives...)

Even if one loses one's wealth, the fact that we have benefited those identified above, should keep us without guilt. It is relevant to recognize the three principal forms of merit—BOON: two circles of closer people (family and friends, of whom the Buddha has talked about many times—e.g., the importance of good friends); savings to be allocated to future necessities—from natural disasters to safety; and important offerings to different groups in society—another recurrent theme in the Buddha's teachings. The ingredients of this path lead us to the expansion of our material and spiritual wealth.

The above can be translated into modern time's policies and programs to strengthen a community or a country's welfare.

One very important consideration is that wealth must not be concentrated in a few hands in our societies, as we witness in the present economic paradigm. It is a well-known fact that globalization accelerated the concentration of material wealth and power. What the Buddha is insinuating here is that there are clear benefits from a more equal distribution of wealth.

Furthermore, this teaching suggests that of all the options listed above, only one important expense in oneself is accepted: one's safety. This means that most of the benefits from wealth derive from benefiting others. As we all know, this is the essence of an egalitarian society, which puts first equity rather than economic efficiency per-se. Protection, support, and enjoyment by others, are essential components of this paradigm on collective human welfare.

This paradigm goes far beyond 'human beings.' In describing the optimal way to address the expenditures that must surge from material wealth, it includes explicitly the expenses that come from offerings to deities; i.e., the offerings to the LIGHT BEINGS.

This is one more example of the Buddha's teachings where economics and spirituality are fully integrated.

In this Sutra, the Buddha concludes something very essential to those of us who are in this spiritual path: *"I have done what will not lead to future distress."* In the language of modern economics, this is often referred to as "negative externalities" of expenditures (private or public). In addition, we should note that the Buddha is referring here to the benefits one receive from our actions; i.e., The Law of Karma and The Right Action from "The Noble 8-Fold Path"—two essential themes in the Buddhist Social Doctrine.

But, it is more than that. The Buddha is very explicit about the actual benefits of an equity-based policy in our societies: *"When this is recollected by a mortal, a person established in the Dharma of the Noble Ones, he is praised in this life and, after death, rejoices in heaven."* In essence, it is stating how material wealth relates to how the Final Judgment will be applied upon us. Thus, it is not all about material satisfaction for material benefits. It is also material wealth management and governance for spiritual benefits.

> **Thus, it is not all about material satisfaction for material benefits**

Chapter 11:

THE MORALITY and ETHICS of POSSESSING WEALTH

(THE APUTTAKA SUTTA)

"The most important human endeavor is the striving for morality in our actions"

Albert Einstein

This text insists in bringing more aspects of wealth creation, conservation and disposition. This section addresses what I call **"THE MORALITY AND ETHICS OF POSSESSING WEALTH".** This is not a new theme, in which the Buddha insist that we have to incorporate in the processes of wealth creation a powerful and meaningful moral and ethics ingredient. This is totally missing in our societies. Materiality is like a horse without slaves.

The presentation here is based on *THE APUTTAKA SUTTA:* Heirless (see translation by Thanissaro Bhikkhu. 1999). Here, a king talks with the Buddha and tells him about a money lender who has recently passed away. A very rich person. Once again, the Sutra presents another context where the Buddha speaks about the use of wealth.

He states: *"When his wealth isn't properly put to use, kings make off with it, or thieves make off with it, or fire burns it, or water sweeps it away, or hateful heirs make off with it. Thus, his wealth, not properly put to use, goes to waste and not to any good use."*

In modern economics, this is discussed under the rubric of the productivity of money. The phrase "put into use" is the one that marks the character of the moral ground around wealth. The Buddha is talking about a 'conscious act.'

This applies also to all forms of capital in a society, including, for example, our natural resources and services of the environment, in recognition of their intrinsic economic value.

The Sutta states:

> *"And, so that water, not properly put to use, would go to waste and not to any good use. In the same way, when a person of no integrity [moral and ethics] acquires lavish wealth...his wealth, not properly put to use, goes to waste and not to any good use... And so that water, properly put to use, would go to a good use and not to waste. In the same way, when a person of integrity acquires lavish wealth... his wealth, properly put to use, goes to a good use and not to waste."*

We have made reference to this in another section of this chapter.

At the end of the Sutra, the Buddha makes this powerful moral statement:

> *"Like water in a haunted place that, without being imbibed, dries up: such is the wealth acquired by a worthless person who neither enjoys it himself nor gives. But one enlightened & knowing, on acquiring wealth, enjoys it & performs his duties. He, a bull among men, having supported his kin, without blame goes to the land of heaven."*

The above is so central to what is happening in the real world today!

Chapter 12:

SOFT SKILLS AS A FORM OF WEALTH. THE 7 TREASURES

(THE DHANA SUTTA)

"If we all did the things we are really capable of doing, we would literally astound ourselves"

Thomas Edison

There is wealth within our inner universe, which we may recognize and apply to the challenges we face in our daily life. In today's jargon, this form of wealth is called "Soft Skills"; they can be explored, developed, and applied. We must conquer that universe and, when necessary, rely on it. For the moment our attention remains focused on different forms of material wealth, coming from our external universe. As we awaken every day, we are fortunate that our inner wealth, our spiritual wealth, is always available to us. We have the opportunity to access this wealth through the practice of Dharma, and the practice of meditation. There are no material limits (e.g., income) to access and expand our soft skills.

Given the above, one might not have money or material wealth, but life may be driven by love, compassion, patience, service, positive thinking, equanimity, joy, etc. This form of capital is sustained by two fundamental pillars: the processes of self-realization and the powers of self-governance. Both are at the disposal of the refinement of our mind; refinement that surfaces through meditation, contemplation, prayer, silence, breathing techniques, yoga... On this path of the refinement of the mind, our Dharma puts at our disposal, for example, the fundamental teachings of "The Four Noble Truths" and "The Noble Eightfold Path". Every instrument to develop our soft skills is contained there. It is vital to begin this path now; an individual path as well as a collective one. A path of merit and unconditional service. To practice them, we do not need to fulfill any pre-condition; only to awaken our inner self.

Thus, it is important to recognize that we possess both "material wealth" and "non-material wealth" (spiritual wealth). It is around the non-material wealth that the Buddha shares with us an endowment of very rich wealth: The Seven Treasures, contained in The Dhana Sutra. As with material wealth, the Buddha also spoke about the urgency of having an ethical foundation for generating, accumulating, maintaining and sharing our inner wealth. Without this ethical foundation, these processes may end-up in mere disasters. We must define how and where to awaken.

The Dhana Sutra begins with a phrase from the Buddha, the great teacher:

> *"Monks, there are these seven treasures. What are they?" the treasure of conviction, the treasure of virtue, the treasure of conscience, the treasure of concern, the treasure of listening, the treasure of generosity, and the treasure of discernment".*

INITIAL COMMENTS

The explanation of these treasures can have many dimensions. The individual dimension and the collective dimension. Each one of us has to take these two dimensions into consideration. All the treasures are interdependent. Sometimes to self-realize one we must self-realize others. This is important for those who chose one, two or three treasures, and for someone who chooses all of them, this represents something very important. Given my knowledge of Buddhism, I think there is a certain hierarchy in the presentation. Certainly the first one is the first. Some others might change their position. For the moment let's see it as hierarchical. What implications does it have for what you have chosen? I would like to acknowledge only one: that everyone should add treasure number one to their lists. As a first step for everyone, we must have a good understanding of the treasures. Study it very well first. As a task we must find the most relevant practices in each case. Treasures also arise as a result of our merits and practices.

THE SEVEN TREASURES

1. THE TREASURE OF CONVICTION:

"Having conviction, and being convinced of the Awakening of the Tathagata (the existence of enlightenment): which translates into dignity and correct awakening, holistically complete in knowledge and conduct, skilled, expert with respect to the world, unsurpassed as a teacher to those people fit to be taught. Being a Teacher of divine and human beings, awakened, and blessed."

There is a unique notion of inner awakening. The Buddha speaks of correct awakening. And, the fundamental principle of correct awakening is the awakening to the reality within the path to enlightenment. This is the reason why it is so important to be familiar with those teachings contained in the Noble Eight-Fold Path (e.g., right vision, right intent...), and the use of the word 'right', which means to contain what it has to contain. To contain everything. Our inner wealth gets awakened within the space of knowledge, wisdom, conduct, habits, skills, the expert, the being of a teacher. The word "correct" is not something moral, but something holistic, complete and wholesome. A complete knowledge. A conduct and habits that correspond to this doctrine, and that have a lot to do with the reality of the world in which we live. A need to be skilled in possessing the intelligent instruments necessary to function daily.

This is the first treasure. Very intriguing when I first read it. But it is of fundamental importance in content and scope. It is the treasure that enables us to follow the right path and to having accumulated our Dharma. Dharma as that body of knowledge and those fundamental spiritual practices which enhance our spiritual life. This is the reason why the Sutra mentions the state of Buddhahood; i.e., the state of enlightenment. In other words, our only horizon and direction towards where we are walking. It is the orientation, it is the map, it is the point of reference... Possessing this form of wealth, this treasure, is a very important for all the treasures that come later on. All the treasures which follow are immersed in this ocean of wisdom.

To follow the right path is fundamental in Buddhism. Understanding the ethics of wealth creation and accumulation is also essential in the establishment of our inner wealth. One is to be inserted within an ethical doctrine which does not ruin our minds (e.g., the enlargement of our ego).

Perhaps it is also relevant to emphasize that "being a teacher" is a necessary element and attribute of our spiritual path. But, one should only teach those who are worthy of this teaching (e.g., those who are ready to respect, understand, practice and self-realize the teachings). This treasure must be understood and meditated-on for a long time until a true synthesis is achieved. It is not trivial.

2. THE TREASURE OF VIRTUE:

"Abstaining from taking life (in every sense), abstaining from stealing, abstaining from illicit sexual conduct, abstaining from lying, abstaining from taking toxic products that cause negligence."

The first thing to understand about this treasure is that the Buddha speaks of "abstaining." The Buddha does not say "abandon," or "withdraw," or "be indifferent to..." Abstaining is a conscious act. To abstain we must know reality as it is. Abstention cannot be born of ignorance. I am speaking of a conscious act to decide not to act or move in a certain direction.

This decision requires the self-realization of several treasures, including the treasure of discernment. Not easy. Right? As you know, this topic of abstention is part of the content and discussion of The Five Precepts (abstaining from taking the life of someone, abstaining from intoxicating oneself...). But we have to understand these precepts very well, particularly their projection.

Abstaining from taking life. In the case of life, it is not just about oneself, or another human being. It is about all manifestations of life, including sentient beings and nature. But there is more: we are fully aware that feelings have life, emotions have life, thoughts have life, illusions have life, attachment has life... And, something even significantly important, that suffering has life.

Here, we have to pause and meditate.

In the case of the other four abstentions (e.g., stealing, illicit sex, intoxicants, and lying) we have to do the same analysis. These are tremendous issues. In the case of stealing, in its original version it is about not taking possession of what is not given to us. Stealing from another person, stealing from future generations, stealing from the planet... But we also steal knowledge, wisdom, without making the necessary efforts to embrace them ethically. There are many people who live with the idea that they have acquired rights.

The same happens with the definition of what is toxic. It is not only about drugs and alcohol. There are many things that intoxicate us, including our own thoughts, values and beliefs. This is a very deep subject, which requires a lot of analysis and decisions. What intoxicates you today? How do you get out of that intoxication?

Finally, the speech, the narrative, the language, the conversation... Just consider that a word will create life or create death. A word can create feelings or can create suffering. A lie can destroy everything.

3. THE TREASURE OF CONSCIENCE:

"Feeling ashamed at the idea of committing physical, verbal or mental misconduct."

You have to have dignity, honor, and modesty in life. I know people who don't care about anything. They don't feel ashamed of anything. They don't even consider the importance or the consequences of their actions. Those who do not reproach their conduct, bad habits... Remember that this treasure speaks of the physical, the mental and the verbal. Three areas of vast impact on our lives.

Everything has become normalized in our societies. There is no longer a standard of measurement, of comparison. Moral and ethical rules have become a hindrance, an inconvenience. There is not a widely accepted moral doctrine.

4. THE TREASURE OF CONCERN:

"Being aware and feeling a concern for the suffering that results from physical misconduct, verbal misconduct and mental misconduct."

The word concern leads us into misunderstandings. There are slogans that people like to use: take care of yourself, don't worry. But I don't want to stay in something semantic. We must get out of this state of total distraction. The monkey mind, the life of a monkey, the action of a monkey. Being aware, concerned, is a wonderful treasure, since it can only arise from conviction, love, generosity, etc. The Buddha is very concrete and explicit. It is about being aware of your bad behavior. A brutal questioning of us. Wake up, it has been said!

The term "physical" requires talking and meditating a little bit more. We may pay more attention to subject matters related to of our body, the importance of our body in the development of our spirituality. Also, we must talk about the subject of health, healing and curing and our spirituality. This implies distinguishing, for example, between medication and meditation, and to strengthening the relationship between health and education.

Negative mental behavior also requires great observations. This raises once again, the question of how to refine the mind? We know that the refinement of the mind is the essence of Buddhism.

5. THE TREASURE OF LISTENING:

"You have listened a lot, you have retained what you have heard, you have stored what you have heard. All the teachings that are admirable in the beginning, admirable in the middle, admirable in the end, which—in their meaning and expression—proclaim the holy life that is completely complete and pure: those that he/she has often heard, retained, discussed, accumulated, examined with his/her mind and well penetrated in terms of his/her views."

It is very interesting how the description of this treasure begins: "Much has been heard"; "Much has been retained"; "What has been heard has been stored." This leads us to ask ourselves many questions: What have we heard?

Have we heard the Dharma? Have we heard what we have to hear? Have we heard the truth? Today, in the world of communications, we have heard too much rubbish. It is important to understand that everything is stored. Therefore, we must ask ourselves: How do we cleanse ourselves of all that?

Finally, listening in the sense of this treasure calls us to a special form of dialogue, which must culminate in our self-realization. This is often called *A Dialogue of Enlightenment*. Let us have dialogues of enlightenment everywhere in the world.

This treasure has a lot to do with The Law of Karma: the formation of a very special form of wealth: our Karmic endowments; i.e., the nature and scope of the relationships with others. Naturally, the question of how to eliminate negative karmas immediately arises.

In this treasure, too, it also appears the concept that the Dharma, the teachings, are "admirable". This raises the question of what is something admirable? Admirable is the marvelous, the astonishing. I like the word astonishment a lot, because sometimes nothing astonishes us. Remember that the Dharma is astonishing at the beginning, in the middle and at the end. This means truth in all its dimensions. It means coherence. It means complete, satisfactory, that it contains everything... It also means that it contains the element of purity and that it is decanted from all contaminating elements.

6. THE TREASURE OF GENEROSITY:

"A conscience cleansed of the stain of stinginess, living at home, freely generous, detached, delighting in being magnanimous, receptive to requests, delighting in the distribution of alms (OFFERINGS)."

This is very nice! But it has a very particular definition, which is worth studying. It speaks of a cleansing process, to begin with. Of all the stains of stinginess. It manifests itself on a personal and global level, passing through the country level. There are many ways of manifesting this stinginess. Let's think about this for a moment.

Furthermore, this treasure raises the question of What does it mean, living at home? Which home is it? For me, being at home means being centered in my Being. In what I truly am.

The Buddha talks a lot about right livelihood. This is said here, because generosity has an origin. The other word used here is to be magnanimous. Here, there are several synonyms to consider: noble, altruistic, selfless, kind... Everything calls us to the fourth noble truth: the path of virtues

Being receptive to requests is a call to equanimity. In generosity there is a clear dimension of equanimity. To achieve justice, equity, equality, solidarity, cooperation... In Chile there is an expression that says: to turn a deaf ear. We are in the era where we are experts in listening without listening. Here there is a clear relationship between the treasure of listening and the treasure of generosity.

Finally, the word alms refers to offerings. There is an interesting passage about the benefits of offering candles: Illuminating the world like a bright light. Not contracting eye diseases; tendency to obtain supernatural knowledge of the divine eye (dibba-cakkhu); having the wisdom to discern good and evil; not appearing clumsy or spiritually dark; less likelihood of being confused and deceived by external conditions; avoiding rebirth in a place of darkness and fatuity; obtaining great karmic blessings; ascending to the heavens, especially the Trayastrimsa Heaven, after death; and rapid realization of nirvana

7. THE TREASURE OF DISCERNMENT:

"Being insightful (perceptive), endowed with discernment of arising and passing away (Impermanence and other laws), noble, penetrating, leading to correct cessation of stress (suffering. Third Noble Truth)."

Tremendous treasure to know that we potentially have all this. Patanjali called it VIVEKA.

Two Sutras are important here, to expand the explanation of this great weakth and asset: discernment. One, *THE SANGITI SUTTA*, or known as "The Discourse For Reciting Together", and two, *THE SARIPUTTA SUTTA.*

In *THE SANGITI SUTTA*, the Buddha distinguishes three types of discernments: coming from listening, coming from thinking and coming developing. Listening, thinking and developing are three fundamental forms of inner capital, which we need to create, develop, reproduce and share. There are too many people, who are very rich in material capital that do not know how to listen, how to think or how to develop. The outcome is often poverty and chaos.

In the *SARIPUTTA SUTTA*, a short and very pointed Sutta text, the Buddha presents other ingredients of inner transformation through discernment, as a form of spiritual capital and as a way to transform oneself in a stream enterer (i.e., commit oneself to the path of true Dharma). The Buddha teaches us about the need to associate with people of integrity as a factor for stream entry. Furthermore, the expansion of discernment happens through the listening to the true Dhamma, the appropriate state of attention (concentration) and the practice in accordance with the Dhamma, is also a factor for stream entry.

The Sutra on *"The 7 Treasures"* (the seven forms of inner spiritual capital) ends as follows:

> *"The man endowed with these is not poor, nor is his life devoid of valuable things. Therefore, he who has a fixed understanding should work diligently to gain confidence, virtue, clarity, and insight into the truth, mindful of the law of one who has understood."*

Chapter 13:

THE RIGHT LIVELIHOODS

"We must not rest until the right livelihood is within reach of every human being upon this earth..."

Agnivesh

Another important area of international debate, today, is "The Right Livelihood" on this planet. A fundamental tenet in Buddhist social doctrine. There are many scientists who hold the view that we have violated the carrying capacity of most ecological systems, and that there is a significant probability that we might be subjected to a major planetary collapse. Some claim that the main cause is excessive population levels and demography, while others claim that is mainly caused by the patterns of socio economic growth and development now in place in most societies.

There are different styles of life and different optional paths to attain higher levels of human welfare. Which one should we collectively choose?

Any debate about livelihood and the future of the planet becomes really unique and meaningful when we self-realize that everything is interdependent; i.e., we depend on each other and we affect each other. In particular, the scope of interdependence resulting from economic actions goes very far in time and space. Just think about global warming and climate change. So, any path we decide to follow will embody gainers and losers as a result. This demands very careful choices, as this is not only about human beings but also about sentient beings and nature. A rather complex task.

One aspect of these choices is to consider that the real essence in economics is not simply materiality and, thus, the debate on livelihood has to go beyond material welfare. We know that most people are longing for happiness, love, joy, equanimity...all of which depend on many important spiritual and non-material factors.

The Buddha was very clear about the true meaning and significance of livelihood, and brought it as a fundamental component of "The Middle Way". Because of our quasi total interdependence, our choices and actions will always have impacts on others. For this reason, the Buddha brought to the fore the ethical dimensions of our individual and collective decisions, and he cautions us with regard as to how we are to live and share within the limited carrying capacity of the planet.

Among the relevant variables at stake (causes and conditions), the Buddha mentions that we need to live in "a suitable locality" and, thus, to ensure the quality of life of all beings. This single policy statement becomes essential in addressing the housing policy of all nations. This unique emphasis on the "quality" of life opens a huge debate on the present and future of humanity.

Within this context, a very comprehensive list of ingredients is to be accounted for in reaching a new consensus about livelihood on this planet, as an organic part of a Buddhist social doctrine. Most ingredients have been presented in various teachings, including, for example:

That societies must improve education and skills to attain higher levels of welfare.

This has been a crucial debate in our modern societies. The relationship between human capital development and the surge of a form of livelihood that is harmonious among all expressions of life. This deserve some minutes of meditation and reflection, where we must understand the importance of human capital development (knowledge, awareness, wisdom, state of the mind, and consciousness at the individual and collective levels) and the welfare for all.

That we are to exercise self-control
(Conscious consumption and Conscious production).
Some go even further: the need to live in a frugal fashion; what
Patanjali called Aparigraha. The point here is to be aware of the
huge and unnecessary wastage of valuable resources to sustain out-
of-question forms of livelihood: excessive hoarding, unnecessary accumulation, bloated consumption, immense production of wastes... In
most cases, if someone is better off, many people, sentient beings and
nature may end up being worse off.

That we have to take into account not only
Human beings but all beings on the planet.
This is a recurrent theme whose principal understanding is that
all forms of life are on the way to enlightenment. Everyone is in
a constant material and spiritual evolution. The fundamental teaching
is that we will never be able to get enlightened if other beings and
sentient beings are constrained to walk that path. I will never be able
to get enlightened if the path we choose results in the suffering of, for
example, our animals.

That society has to take care of the elders
and the children and future generations.
A fundamental issue in Social Buddhism and in establishing the
foundations of social security, social welfare, in our societies.
There is a great concern about the future of our elders. As one may
be preoccupied with the right livelihood of children, the youth and the
adults, there is also serious concerns about the aging. The process of
aging today is correlated with a process of material impoverishment,
inadequate health services, housing and entertainment.

That we have to follow a moral conduct and to practice merits
through economic actions and not let just the market decide
the outcomes of human welfare.
The Buddha was extremely aware that this was fundamental issue with multiple implications and impacts. The moral conduct
surges from our interdependence; from our empowerment at the collective level; and from existing culture, customs, habits and ingrained
beliefs and values which determine our decisions. Market values are
not the ones that have to define the future of our society, particularly,
as it pertains to our common public goods (i.e., which belongs to all
beings.)

That there is a need to adopt a model of "Noble Living" which responds to a different set of values - like love and kindness, frugality - which leads to a simple livelihood.

This concept embraces a set of values that makes the livelihood "noble". Values with regard to our decisions and actions which affect us as well as every form of life. The term noble spark several dimensions of our everyday life: serving others, be in gratitude, embrace meaning and grace in action, prepare to heal the body, mind and soul, and being present in the practice and self-realization of all existing spiritual laws.

That we all have to adopt & self-realize the true value of "equanimity".

This is present in all Buddha's teachings: UPPEKKA. This is a virtue that influences all other virtues and their self-realization. Even love, compassion, etc. It is a capacity to observe and understand all aspects of a particular situation without judgements, without pre-conceived ideas, and without forcing a specific decision or outcome. It is not a passive state of reality; on the contrary, it demands a very active and mindful commitment to life.

**The Buddha presents us a road to everyday living:
METTA (love and kindness),
KAROUNA (compassion),
MUDITA (Sympathetic joy)
and UPPEKKA (equanimity).**

That we are to set norms regarding how wealth is to be obtained.

This is the most important theme in this new millennium. The first challenge is to define the meaning of wealth; e.g., material and spiritual wealth. The norms of how this wealth is finally obtained is the fundamental element of economics and politics today. There is the general claim that wealth surges from very low levels of individual and collective consciousness. Low levels of vibration and thus of self-realization of higher and higher levels of transcendental being and becoming.

That countries must stop trade on drugs and other substances, women or children, toxic substances... An essential guide to competitiveness.

Today we witness the trade of women and children everywhere. We see how drug trade and social penetration is ruining many societies, either developed (rich) or under developed (poor). Drug dealers control most institutions at the private and public levels of decision making. Toxic substances are destroying the quality of our food and nutrition intakes, debilitating the mere essence of humanity. It is as if we are numbed and do not have the ability to know reality like it really is.

That we must practice a form of economics that dispels all forms of suffering.

A major source of suffering comes from today's faulty practices of economics, politics, social and institutions. Economics is guided by the practices of competition and exclusion, all defined by the level of purchasing power of those in the market. Market prices do not reflect the values of goods and services, particularly of those goods that we hold in common (climate, oceans, glaciers, biodiversity...). People suffer as a consequence of economic policies and practices. People suffer because of pollution, poverty, misery, disempowerment, marginalization, loss of identity and sense of belonging...

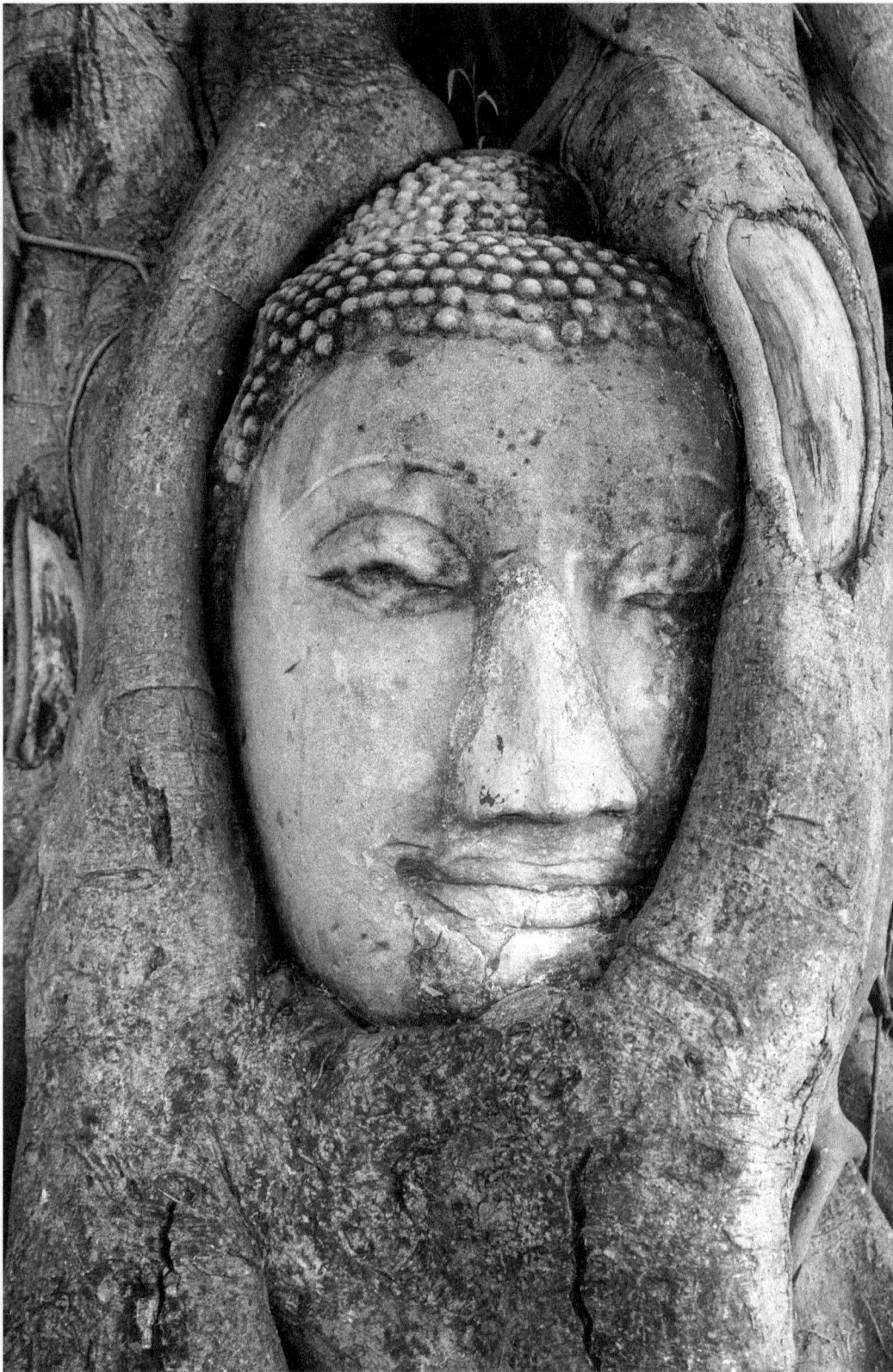

Chapter 14:

BUDDHA &
THE ENVIRONMENT I

(THE KUTADANTTA SUTTA,
THE KARANIYA METTA SUTTA)

"One of the first conditions of happiness is that the link between man and nature shall not be broken"

Leo Tolstoy

The Buddha established the foundations of both inner and outer ecology. If it was dark outside it was not possible to be enlightened inside and vice-versa (following "The Law of Correspondence": the inner is like the outer and the outer is like the inner). Within this context, there are many discourses of the Buddha, in which several principles and spiritual values are taught with the view to heighten many principles about how important nature and ecology are to our human material and spiritual transformations.

The Bodhisattva Path, one of the principal paths and life options in Buddhism is all about the "other": human beings, sentient beings and nature. Thus, many of the Bodhisattva practices have to do with the respect and protection of nature in their several forms.

Buddhism is engulfed by a series of principles essential to be understood, practiced and self-realized. Let us focus on some of them, to illustrate.

One, **NON-VIOLENCE**, which excludes all forms of violence—emphasis added to the violence to sentient beings. This is simply not acceptable.

Two, **ABSTENTION** from taking life to all living beings, including nature. When it is referred to killing, Buddha is also including the decimation of ecological systems. It is also referred in the context of another abstention: not to steal, not to take away, not to misappropriate, etc. of something that has not been given to us. This is important to consider at the individual as well as the collective level.

Three, **INTERCONNECTEDNESS**, which states that everyone and everything are all totally interconnected and interdependent. This means that my transformation and evolution depends on the evolution and transformation of all manifestations of life. And as stated above, it also means that all sentient beings and nature are evolving towards the state of enlightenment. A major process of co-evolution.

Four, **NON-DOMINANCE**, in which no form or manifestation of life should dominate the other forms. We all belong to a matrix of life to contribute to the oneness of its totality, to its unified integration. It is fundamental to promote and practice the respect for al manifestations of life. There is no separability among them. In fact, separability from nature means no real enlightenment for human beings.

All those ingredients stated above contribute to the construction of what HH Lama Gangchen Rinpoche called A NEW ECO-MORALITY; an important theme of this entire book.

In *THE KUTADANTTA SUTTA* there is an interesting debate about the traditions whereby people sacrifice animals as offerings to the gods. There is an extensive discussion and very relevant teachings of the Buddha regarding why NOT to kill animals as offerings, even if one is offering to the highest possible enlightened beings. Other offerings were suggested. This shows the importance that sentient beings, and animals in particular, have for the Buddha.

THE KARANIYA METTA SUTTA, a very short, but powerful text, is devoted to the essence of love and kindness—*METTA*. It has many passages stating the importance of the interconnectedness that exists among all forms of life. In this Sutra this reality is put up front. Let me quote a couple of verses:

> *"Just as with her own life*
> *A mother shields from hurt*
> *Her own son, her only child,*
> *Let all-embracing thoughts*
> *For all beings be yours.*
> *Cultivate an all-embracing mind of love*
> *For all throughout the universe,*
> *In all its height, depth and breadth —*
> *Love that is untroubled*
> *And beyond hatred or enmity."*

In many instances, when some disciples complained about animals disturbing or attacking them during meditation in a quiet place within nature, the Buddha stated two major teachings: (a) the main cause and condition has to do with your karmic debts and imbalances (the degree of friendship with your karma and karmic debts) and (b) the need to go back to nature and apply love and kindness to all creatures (including the sneaks).

The key conclusion is that:

"It is through METTA that there will be peace among all manifestations of life".

Chapter 15:

BUDDHA &
THE ENVIRONMENT II

(THE VANAROPA SUTTA,
THE SARVAGUNAPUNYAKSHETRA SUTTA)

"The earth will not continue to offer its harvest, except with faithful stewardship"

John Paul II

Many people recognize *THE VANAROPA SUTTA (SAMYATA NIKAYA)*, "Discourses With the Devatas"— translated by Bhikkhu Bodhi, as the fundamental thinking of the Buddha on the environment and sustainable development. It a surprisingly short Sutta in length, but tremendously profound in content.

This Sutta is also known as "The Planters of Groves"; a title that possesses multiples connotations.
The Sutta states the following:

> *"For whom does merit always increase,*
> *Both by day and by night?*
> *Who are the people going to heaven,*
> *Established in Dhamma, endowed with virtue?"*
> *"Those who set up a park or a grove,*
> *The people who construct a bridge,*
>
> *A place to drink and a well,*
> *Those who give a residence:*
> *"For them merit always increases,*
> *Both by day and by night;*
> *Those are the people going to heaven,*
> *Established in Dhamma, endowed with virtue."*

The Sutta begins with a description of an ideal horizon for those of us on the Buddhist spiritual path.

First, it mentions the importance of merits. To do merits all the time. But, the type of merits that always increases our level of consciousness and our capacity for self-realization. And, it makes reference to do merits all the time: day and night.

Second, it mentions the need to be established in Dharma, which has a very important meaning. One of them is to be established in the truth of the Buddha's teachings, and to be on the path of our unique mission in this lifetime. A life of constant merits!

Third, it mentions the essence of the path that leads to the elimination of suffering: the practice of virtues *(Metta)*.

All of the above is mentioned with the view to know how and when one is at that point in life. A position, a state of consciousness, within our karmic path. In a direct way, it asks what are the types of merits which makes us virtuous and self-realized. He specifically establishes the practice that will take us human beings to heaven.

That practice is that one which creates the space and time and conditions—THE RESIDENCE—within which those merits give fruits:

1. Those who set up a park or a grove.
2. The people who construct a bridge.
3. A place to drink and a well.

Three very important and practical environmental actions:

First, **Planting, Foresting, and Protecting Environmental Niches.**

These have a larger context today, including the conservation, protection and management of all natural resources and the services of the environment. The connection here goes beyond the material actions; it is directly connected with our process of self-realization and the enlightenment. Without the natural environment, there is no possibility of enlightenment.

Second, **The Construction of Bridges is a Very Important Component of Buddhism.**

In fact, the Buddha talks about this activity several times. His teaching using 'a bridge' is often a metaphor for a number of meritorious acts within our spiritual awakening and karmic path: constructing or repairing all sorts of spiritual bridges.

One example, is in *THE SARVAGUNAPUNYAKSHETRA SUTRA*, in which the Buddha talks about the seven fields of merits (remember what was said above). The fourth and the fifth fields of merit address the importance of bridges:
(i)'maintaining ferries to help people cross rivers' and (ii) 'constructing bridges so that the ill and weak can cross the rivers.'

As it has always been a merit to carve wood or stones to make a Buddha statue, building bridges has been a major spiritual offering in Buddhism. To me, this is one of the most explicit statements and actions to exalt the importance of human and nature interdependence. Building bridges between our material and non-material reality, the inner and the outer, the individual and the collective, the seen and unseen, etc. are to be seriously considered.

Third, A Place Where We Can Drink Water and a Place Where We Experience the Source of Water.

Here, again, the Buddha presents several dimensions of our spirituality in relationship to and with water. Water is one of the fundamental elements of life.

1. Water as the process of purification.
   This is a very powerful spiritual statement.

2. Water as the manifestation of patience and humbleness.
   The water in a still lake.

3. Water as a vehicle of spiritual transformation.
   This is mainly the water of rivers and cascades.

4. Water as a key to our interdependent impermanence.
   Water is never the same as it moves from one state to the other.

5. Water as an offering to all the manifestations of the Buddha.
   Offerings of purification as well as water for bathing.

6. Water as the ever-constant form but ever-changing reality.
   You stand in the middle of a river, the river appears to be the same, but it is never so.

7. Water in the inner and outer ecology, as One.
   The dialogue among the five elements of life: the inner is like the outer and the outer is like the inner.

8. Water that runs under the bridges of mutuality and care.

9. Water that heals the mind, body and speech.

10. Water that deeply transforms our spiritual path and takes away what it is not necessary.

11. The power of water to clean and cleanse.

Chapter 16:

THE FOUNDATIONS OF SOCIAL POLICY

(THE SALEYYAKA SUTTA, THE SIGALOVADA SUTTA,THE MAHAMANGALA SUTTA)

**"Start by doing what's necessary;
then do what's possible;
and suddenly you are doing the impossible"**

St. Francis Of Assisi

During the course of his life, the Buddha created and developed a series of monastic societies. After a careful reading of several sutras, it appears that these societies were rather large and, therefore, it was important to promote social cohesion and stability. Within this context, it is no surprise to find the Buddha speaking about what I believe are different ingredients of a local and national "Social Policy".

One may also seriously consider as part of a Social Policy what is contained within the Vinaya (e.g., responsibilities, habits, merits, engagement, commitment). A theme not treated in this chapter.

Here, the attention is on what he said in *THE SALEYYAKA SUTTA* and a number of other sutras listed below. As it has been most of the time, the presentation focuses on what should be avoided in a societal sense; i.e., on what one should abstain or what should not be done. The general title of these ingredients is known as "The Ten Negative (Unhealthy) Actions"—*KAMMA PATHA*.

Perhaps it is worth stating two broad attributes of this comprehensive understanding of the nature and scope of Social Policy, even before listing in detail the actions to be avoided.

First, That the Social Policy Stated by the Buddha Goes Far Beyond Human Beings, As it is in Today's Social Paradigm. The Policy Extends to All Forms and Manifestations of Life.

Thus, no separation exists among human beings, sentient beings and nature. It is truly noble to understand social policy as including animals and nature in general. In other words, the Buddha's understanding of what constitutes a social policy is the fruit of many spiritual laws; e.g., the law of interdependence, the law of karma, the law of correspondence. The policy prescription is an impossibility to separate any given policy whereby the potential impacts for human beings may be good, while the impacts on animals are bad. Thus, one must not create a social policy that make human beings "better off" while making animals "worse off". In modern language, one must not separate social policy from environmental policy.

Second, That Social Policy Must Include the Inner and the Outer Reality at the Same Time. For The Buddha, 'Social' Includes All Possible Expressions of the Means of Communications and Speech, as Well as the State of the Human Mind (Consciousness), Individually and Collectively.

This is to say that social psychology, behavioral sciences, and collective cognitive experiences are also organic parts of a social policy. These dimensions of what constitutes "social" are much more comprehensive and inclusive than the ones embraced and implemented to date. The new social paradigm proposed here goes into the recognition, understanding and practice of the truly essential causes and conditions determining the social reality we live into today.

The Buddha groups "The Ten Negative Actions" into three broad categories: Body, Speech and Mind.

The ones related to the body, are almost identical to some of the abstentions the Buddha proclaim somewhere else:

(i) Taking the life of living beings *(PANATI PATA)*, (ii) Appropriating something that does not belong or has not been given to us *(ADDI-NADANA)*, and (iii) Misconducting ourselves sexually *(KAMESU MIC-CHACHARA)*.

These must be understood in a very broad sense. Thus, we must consider all forms of killing and stealing. A country that uses 3-5 planet earth to maintain its level of material welfare—when there is only one planet earth—is a major act of stealing. When the foods are contaminated with herbicides, pesticides, hormones, additives, addictive substances... is a major act of killing.

The ones related to the speech involve four extended issues regarding another major abstention - the wrong speech:

(i) false speech *(MUSAVADA)*,
(ii) defamatory speech *(PISUNAVACA)*,
(iii) coarse speech *(PHARUSA VACA)* and
(iv) idle chattering *(SAMPHAPPLAPA)*.

These are key ingredients, particularly, within the political arena of a social policy, which is greatly influenced by communications. The 'social grammar' and the 'narratives' in politics have become essential to determine social stability and cohesion. Speech leads to behavior and behavior leads to actions.

The ones related to the mind are fundamental with respect to deciding what is the right social path in any given society:

(i) the wrong view *(MICCA DITTHI)*,
(ii) ill will or malice *(VYAPADA)* and
(iii) greed *(ABHIJJA)*.

Given the fact that the Middle Way is fundamentally constructed through the Right View, this group is to be seriously understood before designing a social policy for a community, a country and the planet at large.

In *THE SIGALOVADA SUTTA*: The Discourse to Sigala (translated by Narada Thera. 1996) the Buddha brings **THE CODE OF DISCIPLINE** within a given social policy. In other words, this teaching represents the way in which an individual must be prepared to contribute to the collective nature of his or her social reality.

There is a rather long list of "rights" and "wrongs" in relation to human behavior and its consequences. The emphasis here is on two aspects of those teachings only.

First, It Refers to the Ways People May Acquire Wealth (Something We Referred To Earlier). One is to Be Wise and Virtuous in Acquiring Wealth, Including Harmless Ways.

This form of acquisition will lead to a pattern of expenditure which will bring benefits for an entire life: *"One portion for his wants he use—basic needs; two portions on his business spends—wealth expansion, and the fourth for times of need he keeps—hendging one's future."*

Second, It Refers to One Who Contributes to the Collective Social Environment: Hospitable, Friendly, Unselfish...With an Emphasis in Being a Coach, Leader or Instructor.

These are forms of individual identities which are essential to social cohesion and stability. Furthermore, the Buddha brings about a series of skillful means of social empowerment: generosity, sweet speech, helpfulness and impartiality to all (equanimity once again). The conclusion is that empowerment makes the world go around.

A SPECIAL ATTENTION TO THE MAHAMANGALA SUTTA

THE MAHAMANDALA SUTTA is the Sutra of Blessings; of the significant and transcendental blessings (translation from Pali by Narada Thera. Access to Insight. 1994). At first sight, this Sutra as a collection of approximately 40 personal advices, for a correct individual behavior. However, here we inquire into this Sutra from a societal point of view. Perhaps, the first time this has been done systematically.

The presentation of this Sutra must begin with a brief explanation of the meaning of "blessings". Because Mangala is often translated as auspicious and successful (the right path), one may think that the term blessings means something that we are lucky to receive from someone. However, after careful reading, these blessings are the result of the right intent, right language, right action, right behavior, right effort. There is nothing here that is random. The essence that needs to be understood is that we will receive blessings out of our decisions and actions. It is the nature and the quality of those which will create the conditions for the arising of blessings. In social terms, this means that a society must organize itself around The Noble Eight-Fold Path, understand, practice and self-realize each aspects of the path and, as a result it will receive many fundamental blessings. Thus, these blessings are in many ways associated and the result of habits, behavior, social harmony, consensual direction, and a desire of attaining the right livelihood as a collective.

This is the type of Sutra that on face value it is easy to read and have a beginning understanding of what it tries to convey; but, after further inquire it is rather difficult to fully grasp. In many respects, the Sutra calls for self-governance and for social governance, discipline, a code of ethics, the elimination of the social causes and conditions, and the collective practice of virtues: ethic principles that establish the foundations of a Social Doctrine. This doctrine demands a more enlightened way to understand our collective path.

As stated above, the Maha Mangala Sutra contains around 40 components of this Social Doctrine. It is not the objective of this presentation present them one-by-one, but rather to focus on some of the most important ingredients of a Social Doctrine, to feed into the identification and design of social policies.

First, the Buddha recognizes that our societies have the option to choose between accumulating wisdom or simplistic or foolish knowledge and practices. This is why Buddha emphasizes the importance of social discernment, and the importance to associate with the wise and not the foolish. This has direct bearing into the establishment of education and what constitute the essence of learning.

Second, essential to social policy is the family as the most vital cell in a society: the importance of parents, children, wives, husbands. This is particularly relevant in a world today within which the family, family ties, family obligations are crumbling down as a result of individual materialism, competition, exclusion, and social disintegration.

Third, the need for decent work for all, including the notion of peaceful commercial activities, free of conflicts. Here the Buddha recognize the violence embedded in some forms of economic and institutional practices, extremely prevailing in today's societies. One form of violence is hoarding and, thus, the emphasis on giving.

Fourth, a society that does not intoxicate itself, not only with toxic substances but also with the wrong speech, wrong actions, trade of human beings. These are vital to consider in the design of social policy in this 21st Century. Communication technology is extremely powerful today, exercising a tremendous influence on what is absorbed at the personal and social level. Toxic speech seems to be widespread everywhere. All of these require rigor, effort, mindfulness, wisdom, commitment, unshakable mind...

Fifth, establish social policies so that societies do not strive constantly for more material wealth. While the Buddha recognizes the power of wealth creation and expenditures, he also warned us of the social and human impacts of excessive materialism; particularly, a materialism that is not accompanied with a wholesome social ethics and morals. This is why it is essential to design social policies in which embrace contentment, patience, humility and abstentions; these must be made explicit.

Sixth, a social policy must not be conceived as outside or running in parallel with the whole Buddhist Dharma: the truth, the teachings, the mission, the organizing principle. This social policy must be geared to avoid the creation and intensification of social suffering; now extremely prevalent in our countries and the world at large. Dharma and social policy must be one. And, as this book shows, King Ashoka is an example that such social policy based on Buddhist Dharma is indeed possible.

Seventh, as in many teachings of the Buddha, social policy must emphasize the right livelihood –to live in an adequate locality– the right place to live. As demographic concentration and urban sprawl is so prevailing in this era of humanity, the quality of housing, neighborhoods, and cities has become deplorable. It is practically impossible to be in contact with nature and to have a sensible spiritual practice; a vicious circle of human deterioration. Furthermore, it is not only about ecological or physical considerations; it demands a place where one may practice the Dharma. This opens a new dimension of livelihood!

Chapter 17:

SOCIETY'S EVOLVING GOVERNANCE

(THE CAKKAVATTI SUTTA, THE MAHASUDASSANA SUTTA)

"Corruption is the enemy of development, and of good governance."

Pratibha Patil

There are two important Sutras which explain the main attributes of governing any society. These attributes are as relevant today as they were at the time of the Buddha. The Sutras are: *THE CAKKAVATTI SUTTA* – "The Wheel Turning Monarch" (Long Discourses 26, version by Bhikkhu Sujato) and *THE MAHASUDASSANA SUTTA* – The King Mahasudassana (Long Discourses 17, version by Bhikkhu Sujato). They have some similitude in content, as they describe the essence of societal governance for stability, prosperity and wealth. They are not easy to explain within the context of today's social, political and economic reality; however, they contain a huge wealth of ideas and applicable propositions.

The idea here is first, to list some of the most important lessons from both Sutras, and second, to end with a general conclusion.

First, There is an Implicit Notion of "Nation State' Although it Appears to be a Huge State in the First Place. This Idea Surges of the Concept of Letting Yourself Within your Boundaries.

And, when referring to boundaries, I refer to the inner domain of governance. Thus, the sutras begin with a statement to that effect: "If you roam inside your own territory [notion of nation state: the clear existence of boundaries], the domain of your fathers [marked by past history, culture and identity], Māra [the devil, the negative social forces, negativities, wrong outcomes] won't catch you or get hold of you [form of governance, nation]".

Second, The Foundation of Governance has a Direct Correlation with Some Endowments (called "Treasures"). This is a Very Important Component Within the Present Debate on Governance.

Here, it is important to play a little bit with the language and situation of the teaching, 2600 years ago. The seven treasures spelled out in the Sutra are: the wheel (knowledge), the elephant (strength), the horse (social psychology), the jewel (entrepreneurship), the woman (feminine energy), the treasurer (savings and endowments), and the counselor (human capital).

Third, There is an Important Distinction Regarding how to Improve Governance to Attain Better Outcomes. It is Said that Some are to be Earned & Others are Conferred by Lineage (linked to our past).

I assume that attributes like cultural heritage are gained by lineage: to follow our ancestors. With the same token, I also assume that knowledge, strength and entrepreneurship have to be earned, as there may be other ingredients that are fruit of both lineage and earnings.

Fourth, Governance Must Be Guided by Some Determinant Principles. In this Respect, the Sutras Bring About at Least Two Considerations.

(i) 'well then, my dear, relying only on principle—honoring, respecting, and venerating principle, having principle as your flag, banner, and authority—provide just protection and security for your court, troops, aristocrats, vassals, brahmins and householders, people of town and country, ascetics and brahmins, beasts and birds [it is crucial to see the extent of governance as it includes sentient beings]; and (ii) do not let injustice prevail in the realm.

Fifth, There is a distinction between a moral obligation and charity in governing a nation.

This is why the Sutra states that: provide money to the penniless in the realm (paying back a loan, serving honored guests, paying wages, or supplying provisions for essential workers to do their job). It is, thus, more about fulfilling a moral obligation of fairness than offering charity.

Sixth, Governance has several aspects which were repeated everywhere the "monarch" travelled within his kingdom (inside the boundaries).

Do not kill living creatures. do not steal; do not commit sexual misconduct; do not lie; do not drink alcohol; and maintain the current level of taxation. Two aspects must be emphasized: the protection of sentient beings ad nature, and the need for a fiscal policy—governance is not cost free. The latter is expressed as maintaining the level of taxation. It is also an expression of how governance has to deal with equity.

Seventh, Buddha's teaching also refers to the inevitable spiral of negative social, economic and political consequences as a result of poor governance.

Herewith a slim summary of the nature and scope of that spiral:

• **POVERTY.** He provided just protection and security, but he did not provide money to the penniless in the realm, ensuring citizens have enough to live on is not merely a matter of kindness and common decency, but is crucial to ensure stability and national unity. And, so, poverty grew widespread.

• **THEFT.** When poverty was widespread, a certain person stole from others, with the intention to commit theft. In one case the monarch condone the theft providing start-up money, and said: 'with this money, mister, keep yourself alive, and provide for your mother and father, partners and children.' And, added 'work for a living, and establish an uplifting religious donation for ascetics and Brahmins that's conducive to heaven, ripens in happiness, and leads to heaven **(HOW TO SPEND MONEY).**' But, it adds" 'simply providing money is not enough, nor is simply expecting that people can just work for what they want. they need something to get started, together with the support and opportunity to build a life for themselves'

• **THE SWORD.** 'From not providing money to the penniless, poverty became widespread. When poverty was widespread, theft became widespread. When theft was widespread, swords became widespread. When swords were widespread, killing living creatures became widespread. And for the sentient beings among whom killing was widespread, their lifespan and beauty declined.

• **LYING.** 'From not providing money to the penniless, poverty, theft, swords, and killing became widespread. When killing was widespread, lying became widespread. and for the sentient beings among whom lying was widespread, their lifespan and beauty declined.

• **SEXUAL MISCONDUCT.** 'From not providing money to the penniless, poverty, theft, swords, killing, lying, and backbiting became widespread. When backbiting was widespread, sexual misconduct became widespread. And for the sentient beings among whom sexual misconduct was widespread, their lifespan and beauty declined.

• **THE WRONG SPEECH.** 'Two things became widespread: harsh speech and talking nonsense. At this point, the three factors of wrong action—killing, stealing, and sexual misconduct—are present, as are the four factors of wrong speech—lying, backbiting, harsh speech, and nonsensical speech

• **WRONG VIEW.** 'Wrong view became widespread. This completes the three factors of unskillful thought: desire, ill will, and wrong views (which are a strong form of delusion). Here wrong view probably means moral nihilism.

• **IMMORALITY.** 'Among the people, three things became widespread: illicit desire, immoral greed, and wrong custom. Customs or beliefs that legitimize immorality.

• **DISRESPECT.** 'Among the people, these things became widespread: lack of due respect for mother and father, ascetics and Brahmins, and failure to honor the elders in the family.

• **SOCIETAL COLLAPSE.** 'From not providing money to the penniless, all these things became widespread poverty, theft, swords, killing, lying, backbiting, sexual misconduct, harsh speech and talking nonsense, desire and ill will, wrong view, illicit desire, immoral greed, and wrong custom, and lack of due respect for mother and father, ascetics and Brahmins, and failure to honor the elders in the family. for the sentient beings among whom these things were widespread, their lifespan and beauty declined.' 'The ten ways of doing skillful deeds will totally disappear, and the ten ways of doing unskillful deeds will explode in popularity.'

• **PROMINENT RESULTS.** 'The world is protected from this by conscience and prudence. The world will become dissolute, like goats and sheep, chickens and pigs, and dogs and jackals. They'll be full of hostility towards each other, with acute ill will, malevolence, and thoughts of murder.'

The Buddha also shows us a virtuous spiral of growth and development. Let us bring the principal elements of such spiral. Herewith some passages from *THE MAHASUDASSANA SUTA:*

• **THE TERRITORY.** 'You should roam inside your own territory, the domain of your fathers. Doing so, you will grow in life span, beauty, happiness, wealth, and power.

• **PROTECT SENTIENT BEINGS.** The king said,
"Do not kill living creatures. do not steal. do not commit sexual misconduct. do not lie. do not drink alcohol. maintain the current level of taxation."

> *"So that's what they do. Because of undertaking this skillful thing, their lifespan and beauty will grow. Those people who live for ten years will have children who live for twenty years."*

To end, it is relevant to emphasize the comprehensive nature of the social policy suggested by the Buddha. This includes all beings, and not only human beings, and a series of realizations with their skillful means, which are to be taken into account.

The Buddhist ethical principles are essential for the well functioned human society.

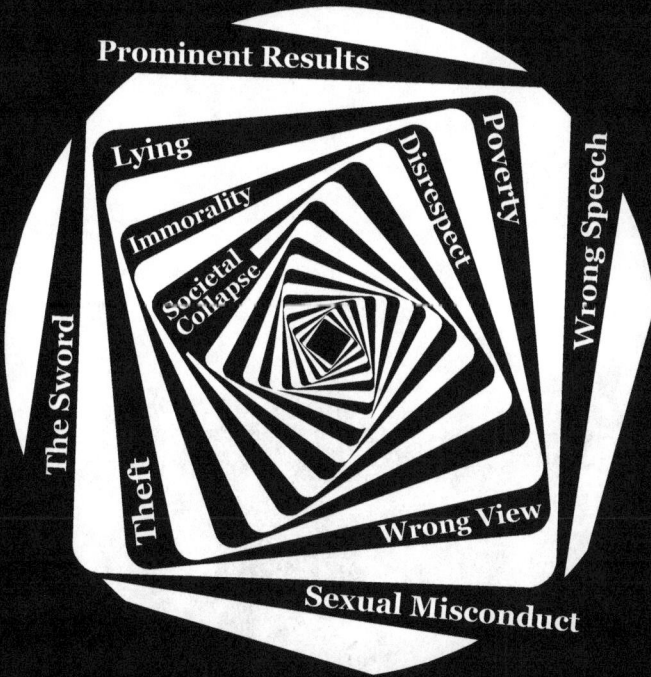

Chapter 18:

BUDDHISM & HUMAN RIGHTS: Some Initial Remarks

"To deny people their human rights is to challenge their very humanity"

Nelson Mandela

Today, there are infinite debates on human rights everywhere; particularly, on human rights violations. These debates may be related to civil and political considerations; economic, social and cultural considerations, or to overall development considerations.

After years of participation in the international debates on human rights, I realize that it is a rather complex topic, and it demands quite a lot of knowledge and dedication. For this book, I have selected two fundamental questions: (i) Is the issues of rights a relevant issue to Buddhists (whose rights may be being violated) and is there a unique form of engagement as Buddhist within their societies, and (ii) What did the Buddha teach us within this realm, specifically and explicitly, on this issue of human rights, the rights of sentient beings and the right to nature, and the right to development?

In principle, we may agree that the first question is extremely important in the realm of integrating Buddhists and Buddhism into our societies, where they face complex social, institutional and political realities. Within this context, it seems that the answer to the second question may be somewhat controversial; not to me, but to some Buddhists who state that the Buddha never talked about human rights proper. Thus, the topic of human rights in Buddhism must be taken carefully and responsibly.

This chapter focuses on what it may seem as a series of disparate themes although in the end, the treatment of these themes will set some foundation for what follows later on in this chapter. Patience is of essence here, as it is impossible to determine how much the reader knows of human rights, as addressed in our societies and in the world at large (i.e., the jurisprudence and justiciability of the different forms of rights).

> **Human rights surge mainly because, or as a result of our quasi-totally interdependent reality**

To start, we must understand that human rights surge mainly because or as a result of our quasi-totally interdependent reality. As it has been said so many times in this book, the structure of our interdependent nature of our reality is the most salient characteristic within the material world we live today. This means that all I do will affect someone else. It is difficult to find examples of actions that are really neutral with regard to others, in a material sense, or actions that are "karmic neutral" in a spiritual sense. Only enlightened beings are karmic neutral.

All basic human conditions –food and nutrition, housing/shelter and livelihood, etc.—within a world of material scarcity, are leading to competition, hoarding greed, power seeking and much more. These affect the reality, 'territory' and freedom of others. This raises another fundamental question: How one is to be protected, or should one be protected, from the potential violations of our basic path to higher levels of consciousness and quality of life? This question raises the idea that we should not be constrained by others in our spiritual development and capacity to reach higher levels of consciousness. Evidently, this should not be allowed, even in the construction and management of monastic societies.

Furthermore, it is becoming increasingly difficult to live in a world where the most relevant assets are held in common, like our global and national goods and services: climate, biodiversity, clean air and water, glaciers, safety, security, migration, natural disasters, oceans and rivers... As it is extremely well known, the mismanagement of these goods will lead to a major collective tragedy for humanity. Some rules of the game should serve to avoid such a tragedy. These are called rights and shared responsibilities.

To add, the embracement of ethics and morals in our societies (not to kill, not to steal, not to get intoxicated, not to trade women and children...), which should not be violated, also have become part of an important scaffold of rights and responsibilities. The violation of those rights has consequence on others, and they have to be addressed in order to avoid them in the first place. Positive and negative incentives and rewards are now in place, under the rubric of "justiciability" (i.e., a system of punishment and rewards).

> **Attention to human rights in Buddhism may be considered a very powerful skillful means**

Part of the ethics and morals in our societies has to do with the avoidance of inequalities of all sorts: economic, social, environmental, political. All of which were recognized by the Buddha 2600 years ago. His famous statement about the fact that lower casts could also get enlightened, and not just the Brahmins, is a major recognition that rights exist and that these must not be violated by some odd social norm. This is one of the most powerful statements on the 'right to development.' This book will treat this situation and share how the Buddha addressed it within a concept of 'rights' that had to do mainly with deeds than within which family it happens you are being born. **Thus, the Buddha proclaims "rights born of deeds" and not "rights born out of some predefined privileges".** A preoccupation of not only the rights of Buddhists but also the rights of non-Buddhists as well.

Also, independent of the various formal concepts of human rights (particularly those concepts born in the West), attention to human rights in Buddhism may be considered a very powerful skillful means. For example, the change in our habits is of crucial relevance in the elimination of the causes and conditions of suffering as well as in the practices of such virtues as *Metta, Karouna, Mudita* and *Upekka*. Many of our bad habits provoke violations of one's own rights as well as someone else's rights. Establishing a series of mutual obligations, as it is done in the Vinaya, have become extremely relevant to consider today.

There is a necessity to establish a "Planetary Vinaya". Without these mutual obligations, it will become impossible for humanity to survive. We will see how these mutual obligations surge within the space of the Buddha's teachings and skillful means.

An example of a fundamental mutual obligation is that of not killing other beings; this is essential to attain Buddhahood!

In the descriptions adopted here you may note that some of the fundamental principles to recognize the essence of human rights within Buddhism are treated by others as simple means or mere institutional instruments.

To close the circle of understanding, the ideal presentation must include references to the interconnected relationships among: human nature, human relationships, and human rights. For example, and as a point of departure, some of the people involved in the debate on Buddhism and human rights, are saying that "human rights", as taught in the West, assume that each individual has a separate and independent identity. The only fact that we can say "my rights" and "your rights" is a demonstration that we live somehow in a world of separate identities and, at the same time, of disparate realities. If this is the case, and as an argument against rights in Buddhism, they add that behind the western notion of human rights there is a view and a perception that human beings are essentially selfish beings (me, me, me...).

Perhaps, an exception to this rule is John Rawls' Theory of Justice. There, the main debate is on justice, with rights as mere means of attaining justice. But for him, to focus on justice is to focus on the virtue of fairness; a virtue based mainly on mutuality and interdependence. This is a good return, once again, to the Buddha's teachings, in which reciprocity is an essential ingredient of any possible notion of rights and responsibilities, and it is a fundamental pillar to the Buddha's notion of Social Policy.

The above calls for another relevant consideration: the present debate on rights is revealing that it is immerse in a specific notion of human nature: disturber, greedy, egocentric, indifferent... Thus, individuality becomes de center of the mandala of human life. This positioning has demonstrated to be a disaster. To live in a world of millions of secondary identities separates us in all possible human activities: I am black you are white, I am fat you are thin, I am Chilean you are Nepalese, you are Christian Democrat I am Communist. But, it is not human rights that creates this separation! It is that notion of human nature.

Another notion of human nature is that one which considers mutuality in its maximum expression within the values of reciprocity, equanimity, cooperation, solidarity, compassion, love, justice, etc. To me, the Buddha's sutras express reciprocity everywhere, and this demands rights and duties; for example, the Buddha's statement regarding the relationship between husband and wife.

In today's world, it is impossible to think about human relations without rights and responsibilities, not necessarily in a legal sense. One example is the notion of ethics and the practice of human dignity, within the principle of dependent origination.

> **It is impossible to think about human relations without rights and responsibilities**

In addition, there are points of strong contact between rights and the nature and ability to address the **Five Precepts** *(Panca Sila):*

1.   Not to cut off life (kill)
2.   Not to take what has not been given
3.   Avoid speaking falsely
4.   Abstain from improper sexual activity
5.   Avoid becoming intoxicated

Nobody wants to be limited by another being from self-realizing the Five Precepts! This is not just an individual affair; it is also a collective one.

A similar argument could be established regarding the relationship between rights and responsibilities and The Four Noble Truth. The fundamental question that we have to pose at this very moment is: **Are human rights part of the two paths offered by the Buddha in The Four Noble Truth?** The path towards the elimination of the causes and conditions of suffering and the path to the elimination of suffering (e.g., the practice of essential virtues). It seems essential that we Buddhists say something about how the nature and compliance with human rights may contribute to the cessation of suffering *(DUKKA)*. Even if natural conditions do not permeate the notion of human rights and, thus, understood as a created convention (not governed by Natural Law), it is relevant to note that our human existence is also governed by Human Law and Spiritual Law. It is for this reason that Buddhism has a lot to say and contribute to the national and international debate on human rights and responsibilities. I refer here to all forms of human rights.

The true test of whether or not we should engage in a debate on human rights and Buddhism is not about its conceptual underpinnings, but about what is the Buddhist response when the rights are actually violated.

SOME ADDITIONAL CONSIDERATIONS[13]

There seems to be an essential relationship between the canonical principles and norms, embedded in Buddhist Dharma, and the essential ethical foundations of human rights. In many ways, the essence of any human right is an extension of human nature, with the corresponding reciprocity of human shared responsibilities. One says this, despite of the fact that prominent Buddhist scholars share that there is no word in Pali (the original languages of the written teachings) which conveys directly a western notion of human rights. However, it seems clear that many of the social teachings of the Buddha do explicitly address the potential impacts of violations of human rights and to walk the road towards those violations. One example those teachings is The Five Abstentions, proclaimed by Lord Buddha, like not to steal, not to-kill, not to intoxicate yourself, sexual misconduct and not to lie or use a wrong speech. Furthermore, one could also say that the eight

---

13   This section is based on a review of some important publications:
1.   Uttamkumar S. Bagde, Essential elements of human rights in Buddhism. Applied Microbiology Laboratory, Department of Life Sciences, University of Mumbai, Vidyanagari, Santacruz (East) Mumbai- 4000098, India. May 2014.
2.   Saneh Chamarik, Buddhism and Human Rights Faculty of Political Science Thammasat University Bangkok. (Preamble by Phra Rajavaramuni Payutto. Thai Khadi Research Institute Thammasat University Bangkok, Thailand 1982.
3.   Khem Bun, Buddhism and Human Rights: Gotama Buddha's Contributions to the Development of Human Rights. *Paññāsāstra* University of Cambodia, PUC. Phnom Penh, Cambodia
4.   Robert Traer, Buddhists and Human Rights. Revision of material in Faith in Human Rights: Support in Religious Traditions for a Global Struggle (Washington, DC: Georgetown University Press, 1991).
5.   Damien Keown, Are There "Human Rights" in Buddhism? University of London, Goldsmiths
6.   Damine V. Keown, Charles S. Prebish, and Wayne R. Husted, edited. Curzon Press. 1998, pp. 239.
7.   Thanissaro Bhikkhu, Non-Violence: A Study Guide. Access to Insight (BCBS Edition. 30 November 2013. http://www.accesstoinsight.org/lib/study/nonviolence.html .
8.   Thanissaro Bhikkhu, "Introduction to the Patimokkha Rules". Access to Insight (BCBS Edition), 17 December 2013, http://www.accesstoinsight.org/tipitaka/vin/sv/bhikkhu-pati-intro.html
9.   Unuwaturabubule Mahinda Thero. Universal Declaration of Human Rights and the Buddhist Teaching. Social Sciences and Humanities Review, Volume 02, No. 02, March 2015, ISSN: 2279-3933
10.   FOCUS Articulating Human Rights in the Context of Buddhist Ethics in Sri Lanka. September 1997 Volume 9.
11.   Yoichi Kawada. The Buddhist Perspective of Life and the Idea of Human Rights. Journal of Oriental Studies 30-1: 110.

essences of The Noble Eight-Fold Path are essential in the definition, understanding and applications of various forms of human rights. Not less relevant is the Buddhist path of practicing the important virtues (in modern language: practicing human values). These may include generosity, equanimity, love, compassion, freedom, etc.; all essential to human rights. In sum, the concept of human nature is indeed the ultimate foundation and the ethical grounds of human rights.

There is a number of spiritual laws in Buddhism that are also essential in the construction a solid framework for human rights and the right to nature. One of them is that rights surge from the existence of the Law of Interdependence. We are not an island and, thus, it is vital to norm human habits, behaviors and engagement.Interdependence, and the mutuality it necessitates, is the vehicle through which all beings attain their maximum level of material and spiritual welfare. Also, the well-known Law of Karma acts as a moral code and order in many circumstances. It is within this

> **Rights surge from the existence of the Law of Interdependence**

context that one understands the Buddha elimination of slavery and cast system; e.g., a fundamental road to inner and outer freedom. But, the human rights views of the Buddha opened the meaningful road towards enlightenment to all beings. In essence, the equality among all beings is this access to enlightenment, in spite of our biological, physical, cultural, ethnic, mind-set, consciousness, awareness, wisdom... differences. Thus, a situation where rights are not just an outright form of free will, as we affect each other via interdependence. This notion of equality also serves the purpose to explain that we are all subject to birth, aging, and death. This is like saying that equality is the mirror image of how the Law of Karma is ingrained in all of us.

Understanding human rights within Buddhism also brings about fundamental concepts to our modern western societies. Examples of such concepts are: the right to development and the freedom to self-development. These are *Metta* Human Rights, as none of the existing human rights will be totally implemented without a powerful process of self-development. These two rights have within themselves the essence of what constitutes a Buddhist's ethics. The Buddhist paradigm on human rights goes far from a materialistic view of society. Thus, it is not just about civil and political rights. Buddhism has a lot to say about economic, social and cultural rights and the right to development. Without the foundation described above, the road to equal rights of many societies ends up strengthening a system where the citizens remain unequal. It is there when it is relevant to understand that for human rights to be implemented in their full expression we must create the proper Karmic Context—e.g., the proper causes and conditions for interaction.

Human rights were so relevant to the Buddha that today we have at our disposal a fundamental text entitled: *PATIMOKKHA*. This text contains the rules, norms, regulations, agreed habits, forms of punishment... governing those monastic societies. It includes very specific rights and responsibilities within that society: peace, well-behavior, habits, restraints, preventions, discipline, obligations... These rules go in tandem with the whole practice of the Dharma-related teachings; i.e., these are inseparable. Thus, rights do not become mere expressions of legal norms, rules and regulations. Legality is like a rather inferior state of affairs in the definition and implementation of rights. This recognizes the fact that we are governed by three system of rights: human rights, nature rights and dharma rights. This also says that **we cannot separate any notion of right, responsibility or punishment from the state of the mind.** The training and refinement of the mind (perceptions, discernment, cognitive experience, concentration, awareness) play an essential role in a society governed by rights and responsibilities. To study the *PATIMOKKHA* is essential in this context. It is a rather vast and comprehensive text. It becomes the basis for understanding the Buddhist jurisprudence and justicability; the latter understood as the foundations of punishment.

The training and refinement of the mind play an essential role in a society

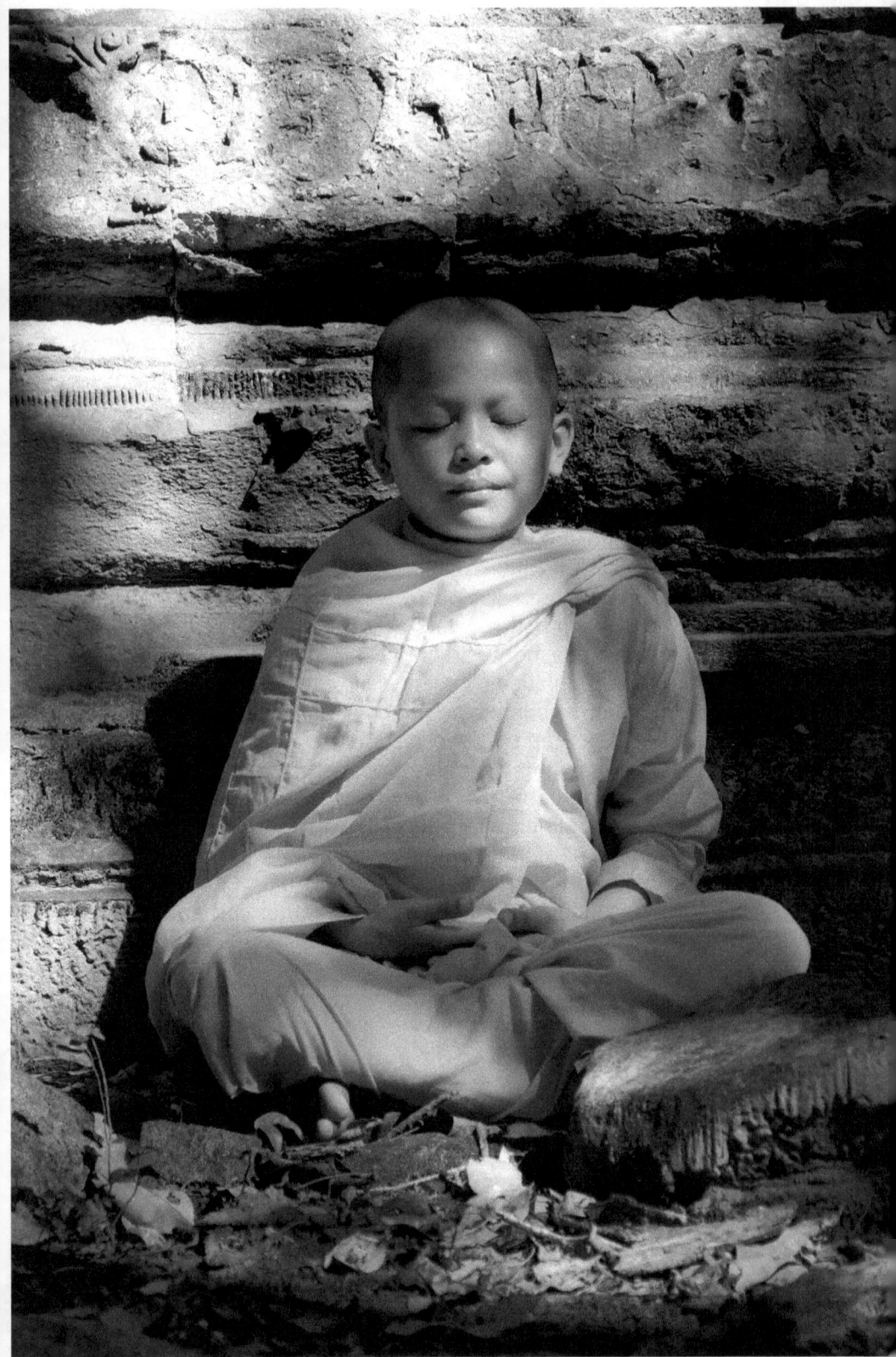

Chapter 19:

BUDDHISM & HUMAN RIGHTS: More Insights

"Injustice anywhere is a threat to justice everywhere"

Martin Luther King Jr.

The Buddha talked about various forms of rights (not only human rights), and he established first, the universal foundations of those rights, to be applied in any society, person, sentient being and nature. These foundations were pre-conditions to the existence of rights as well as to the implementation of those rights. In this respect, this universal foundation was sustained, among many other attributes and frameworks by, for example, **The Brahma Viharas** [*METTA* (LOVE), *KAROUNA* (COMPASSION), *MUDITA* (SIMPATHETIC JOY) and *UPEKKA* (EQUANIMITY)], **the Abstentions, The Five Precepts, The Four Noble Truths, the Practices of Virtues, The Noble Eight-Fold Path** and so much more.

Another universal foundation of human rights in Buddhism is The Law of Karma: we are responsible of our actions and their consequences both, over space and time.

Also, and in part, the axis mundi of human rights in Buddhism is anchored into very important spiritual laws (i.e., The Law of Correspondence: the inner is like the outer and the outer is like the inner; The Law of Interdependence: all beings and nature are fully interdependent), which establish a path to even higher levels of human consciousness.

Different from the well-known "Universal Declaration of Human Rights", for the Buddha the notion and framework of human rights must be "extended" far beyond the rights of human beings. The Buddha's framework includes the rights of all manifestations of life on this planet. This is fundamental premise.

Thus, love must be spread to all living beings in all corners of Planet Earth. In the ethics of Buddhism's rights there are no distinctions or forms of discrimination (superior or inferior rights). This is why the Buddha always included the rights of every sentient being and nature.

One should note that the deeper message to be conveyed here is that the rights of human and sentient beings are "co-equal rights", because the true nature of life, in all its manifestation, is co-equal.

The abovementioned dimensions represent a new fundamental point of departure in the national and international debate on rights. In this framework, there are many spiritual principles surging from several sutras, which have something major to contribute to the formation and understanding of human rights; i.e., the nurturing of the Spiritual Jurisprudence and Spiritual Justiciability of Rights.

> **Love must be spread to all living beings in all corners of Planet Earth**

This text has approached first those passages in the Sutras, where the notion of rights is most explicit. The reader will note that even in the first discourse—i.e., *The DHAMMA-CAKKA-PPAVATANA SUTTA*—one finds very important human rights issues to be considered. Whenever appropriate, and for comparison purposes, reference will be made also to the modern understanding of human rights.

It is worth mentioning the need to complement the presentation with teachings that are geared to address, for example, (i) the issue of suffering; both, individual and collective suffering; i.e., when a person suffers the community also suffers and (ii) the teachings of the Buddha on The Right Livelihood; an essential pillar for all forms of human interactions, which define both, rights and responsibilities.

THE CHAKKAVATTI SINHANAD SUTTA

This Sutra begins emphasizing a fundamental condition of human rights: **the quality of GOVERNANCE.** These are clearly stated by the Buddha when he teaches The Noble Duties of a Universal King. Herewith some of these duties:

> *"...relying only on good qualities—honouring, respecting, and venerating good qualities, having good qualities as your flag, banner, and authority—provide righteous protection and security for your people in the mansion, provide righteous protection and security for your armies, provide righteous protection and security for your officers all over the earth, provide righteous protection and security for priests, provide righteous protection and security for all the people, provide righteous protection and security for recluses and provide righteous protection and security for animals and birds. Do not let injustice spread in the kingdom. Give money to the poor in the kingdom."*

The Buddha added a series of questions to strengthen Governance in a community or country: *"What is wholesome? What is unwholesome? What is wrong? What is right? What should be practiced? What should not be practiced? Doing what, leads to my lasting harm and suffering? Doing what, leads to my lasting welfare and happiness?"*

The Sutra concentrates also on the negative impacts on not addressing poverty as part of the noble duties of a king on human rights. Part of the story was related to helping the poor people with appropriate funds and assistance. The king help a group of thieves. The word spread and so many people begun to steal with the view to get assistance from the King. But, contrary to expectations the King punish them. Thus, you cannot benefit from a right by violating another right: stealing from others.

The Sutra describes very graphically the consequences of poverty:

> *"And so, monks, from not giving money to the poor, poverty became widespread. When poverty was widespread, theft became widespread. When theft was widespread, using swords became widespread. When using swords was widespread, killing became widespread, killing became widespread, lying became widespread, when lying became widespread, backbiting became widespread, when backbiting became widespread, sexual misconduct became widespread. When sexual misconduct was widespread, harsh speech and idle chatter became widespread, when harsh speech and idle chatter became widespread, craving for others' belongings and anger was widespread, when craving for others' belongings and anger became widespread, wrong view was widespread, when wrong view was widespread, excessive lust, immoral greed, and wrong beliefs became widespread, when excessive lust, immoral greed, and wrong beliefs became widespread, not taking care of mother and father, lack of respect for recluses, teachers and the elders in the family was widespread. Because these things were widespread, their lifespan and beauty declined."*

The Buddha then turn to the monks and make reference to several dimensions of their life:

> *"And what is long life for a monk?*
> *"And what is beauty for a monk?*
> *"And what is happiness for a monk?*
> *"And what is power for a monk?*
> *"And what is wealth for a monk?*

I would like to refer here to this latter question:

> *"What is wealth for a monk? It's when a monk meditates spreading a heart full of loving kindness to one direction, and to the second, and to the third, and to the fourth. In the same way above, below, across, everywhere, all around. He spreads a heart full of loving kindness to the whole world—abundant, expansive, limitless, free of enmity and ill will. he meditates spreading a heart full of compassion ... appreciative joy ... equanimity to one direction, and to the second, and to the third, and to the fourth. In the same way above, below, across, everywhere, all around, he spreads a heart full of equanimity to the whole world—abundant, expansive, limitless, free of enmity and ill will. This is wealth for a monk."*

All conditions of human rights.

THE RAHULOVAD SUTTA
(MAHARAHULOVADASUTTA)

The beauty of this Sutra is the fact that it is a conversation of the Buddha with his own son. Here, the Buddha gives us several dimensions of human and nature rights.

First, the Sutra focuses on the non-material dimensions of The Right of Nature. It begins with a tremendous description of the five elements of life—the earth element, the water element, the fire element, the wind element and the space element--which must all be taken into account when we talk about The Right of Nature. This Spiritual Jurisprudence opens up a new discussion regarding the nature, scope, and implementation of human rights in modern societies. It is well known that it has been very difficult to embrace and ratify the Right of Nature, nationally and internationally.

But to enter into this debate, we need to add another dimension to the above considerations.

Second, the Sutra focuses on the conditions necessary to recognize, understand and implement the Right of Nature. Specifically, the Sutra links the possibilities to implement such a right to our state of consciousness. This connection brings to the fore the spiritual dimensions of human rights. The Buddha explicitly tells Rahul to pay specific attention to: **FORM, FEELINGS, PERCEPTION, CHOICES AND CONSCIOUSNESS.** These five elements are to be addressed separately and in depth; something which goes far beyond the scope of this book.

To be able to integrate these dimensions of human rights the Buddha offers the power of meditation. But, not just any meditation. It offers one of the most powerful meditation the Buddha ever taught. In essence what the Buddha is saying is that defining rights has a perfect correlate with a unique level of consciousness. Because that level of consciousness is not there, rights are being violated everywhere.

In addition to meditate like on each of the five elements of life, the Buddha tells his son Rahula:

• *Meditate on love.*
For when you meditate on love any ill will will be given up.
• *Meditate on compassion.*
For when you meditate on compassion any cruelty will be given up.
• *Meditate on rejoicing.*
For when you meditate on rejoicing any discontent will be given up.
• *Meditate on equanimity.*
For when you meditate on equanimity any repulsion will be given up.
• *Meditate on ugliness.*
For when you meditate on ugliness any lust will be given up.
• *Meditate on impermanence.*
For when you meditate on impermanence any conceit 'I am' will be given up.

Furthermore, develop the mindfulness of breathing. When mindfulness of breathing is developed and cultivated it's very fruitful and beneficial.

THE VASALA SUTTA

The teachings of the Buddha greatly impacted the understanding and implementation of social rights. This is not the theme of this Sutra only.

One of the most significant revolutions that surged from the Buddha's teachings is the demise of the Cast System in India. Very often, the ideas come up from a very pointed debate with those Brahmins who, by definition, are located in the highest cast. The Vasala Sutra is one of the most prominent examples. This is done through the concept of Lowlife; a term used by one Brahmin to the Buddha.

The Buddha challenged the Brahmin by asking the question: "Do you know what a lowlife is? The answer by the Buddha to that questions shows the most powerful form of Equal Rights, in the material world as well as in the spiritual world.

The Buddha said this:

> "Irritable and hostile, wicked and offensive, a man deficient in view, deceitful: know him as a lowlife.
> He harms living creatures born of womb or of egg, and has no kindness for creatures: know him as a lowlife.
> He destroys and devastates villages and towns, a notorious oppressor: know him as a lowlife.
> Whether in village or wilderness, he steals what belongs to others, taking what has not been given: know him as a lowlife.
> Having fallen into debt, when pressed to pay up he flees, saying 'I don't owe you anything!':know him as a lowlife.
> Wanting some item or other, he attacks a person in the street and takes it: know him as a lowlife.
> For his own sake or the sake of another, or for the sake of wealth, a man tells a lie when asked to bear witness: know him as a lowlife.
> He is spied among the partners Both Norman and Bodhi add a term suggesting transgression here, in line with the commentary and the apparent sense. I don't, as I suspect the text is

corrupt. Could diss be duss?of relatives and friends, by force or
seduction: know him as a lowlife.
Though able, he does not look after his mother and father when
elderly, past their prime: know him as a lowlife.
He hits or verbally abuses his mother or father, brother, sister,
or mother-in-law: know him as a lowlife.
When asked about the good, he teaches what is bad, giving
secretive advice: know him as a lowlife.
Having done a bad deed, he wishes, 'May no-one find me out!'
His deeds are underhand: know him as a lowlife.
When visiting another family he eats their delicious food, but
does not return the honor: know him as a lowlife.
He deceives with lies ascetics and brahmins and other nomads:
know him as a lowlife.
When time comes to offer a meal to brahmins or ascetics, he
abuses them and does not give: know him as a lowlife.
He talks about what never happened, being wrapped up in de-
lusion, chasing after some item or other: know him as a lowlife.
He extols himself and disparages others, brought down by his
pride: know him as a lowlife.
He's a bully and a miser, of corrupt wishes, stingy, and devi-
ous, shameless, imprudent: know him as a lowlife.
He insults the Buddha or his disciple, whether lay or renunci-
ate: know him as a lowlife.
He claims to be a perfected one, when he really is no such thing.
In the world with its Brahmas, that crook is truly the lowest
lowlife. These who are called lowlifes I have explained to you."

All of the above characterizations have to either with an attribute or a direct form of violation of human rights.

But, the most powerful statement on social rights, comes at the end:

"You're not a lowlife by birth, nor by birth are you a brahmin. You're a lowlife by your deeds, by deeds you're a brahmin."

Human rights must be established by deeds!

THE ESUKARI SUTTA

This Sutra shows that it is very difficult to separate rights from responsibilities; they go hand in hand. The essence of the Sutra is a debate on social rights, from the perspective of one cast trying to impose responsibilities and areas of social actions and interventions. At the very beginning the teachings are related to a situation in which the Brahmins impose responsibilities through the segmentations of services that each cast is supposed to perform in any society.

In particular, the Buddha questions as to whether a Brahmin is authorized to create a self-serving structure of rights and responsibilities through what is called the Four Kind of Services: "for a brahmin, an aristocrat, a peasant, and a menial". This is a pyramidal way of providing services, where the Brahmin is served by all others and the menials are only served by themselves. A very deficient way of assigning rights as it creates and intensify more inequality everywhere.

The Buddha destroys this assignment of rights from several angles. First, and as stated earlier, by questioning the social authority of a brahmin. The Buddha ask the following question: "did the whole world authorize the brahmins to prescribe these four kinds of service?" The answer did not wait: *"No, Master Gotama."*

The Buddha characterizes this unequal system of assignment of rights and responsibilities saying:

> *"It's as if they were to force a steak on a poor, penniless person, telling them they must eat it and then pay for it. In the same way, the brahmins have prescribed these four kinds of service without the consent of these ascetics and brahmins."*

In an extremely eloquent way, the Buddha express the kernel of His paradigm: *"brahmin, I don't say that you should serve everyone, nor do I say that you shouldn't serve anyone. I say that you shouldn't serve someone if serving them makes you worse, not better. And I say that you should serve someone if serving them makes you better, not worse."* This is saying also that the assignment of rights should make every one better off and nobody worse off.

In addition, the Buddha ends these arguments with the essence which permits to eliminate immediately the cast system: *"brahmin, i don't say that coming from an eminent family makes you a better or worse person. i don't say that being very beautiful makes you a better or worse person. i don't say that being very wealthy makes you a better or worse person."*

The Buddha adds: *"For some people from eminent families kill living creatures, steal, and commit sexual misconduct. They use speech that's false, divisive, harsh, or nonsensical. And they're covetous, malicious, with wrong view. That's why I don't say that coming from an eminent family makes you an even truer person."*

In addition: *"But some people from eminent families also refrain from killing living creatures, stealing, and committing sexual misconduct. They refrain from using speech that's false, divisive, harsh, or nonsensical. And they're not covetous or malicious, and they have right view. That's why I don't say that coming from an eminent family makes you a worse person."*

Then, the whole debate on rights moves to the issues of wealth, where the same logics apply (like having consent of others). Within this context, the Buddha teaches us that: *"a person's own wealth is the noble, transcendent teaching. But they are reckoned by recollecting the traditional family lineage of their mother and father wherever they are incarnated. If they incarnate in a family of aristocrats they are reckoned as an aristocrat. If they incarnate in a family of brahmins they are reckoned as a brahmin. If they incarnate in a family of peasants they are reckoned as a peasant. If they incarnate in a family of menials they are reckoned as a menial."*

The Buddha also states and grants enlightenment to anyone who is ready to walk that path, independently of a given cast. This is the most revolutionary teaching of the Buddha. In an analogy in which He uses "fire", the Sutra states that: *"The fire produced by the high class people with good quality wood would have flames, color, and radiance, and be usable as fire, and so would the fire produced by the low class people with poor quality wood. For all fire has flames, color, and radiance, and is usable as fire."*

THE ATTADANDA SUTTA

In many ways, the assignment of rights is related to the avoidance of potential conflicts and violence. In particular, social consciousness is such that in the absence of those rights several socially negative impacts will surge in our society. *THE ATTADANDA SUTTA* refers to one important source of violence in our societies: competition with one another. This competition provokes fear, and in fear the world feels without any substance. All of this generates discontent and people "run in all directions".

The above calls for a powerful way of self-governance; something essential for the successful implementation of human rights. This would include the elimination of greed and avarice, conquer laziness, weariness, sloth, ego... Furthermore, the Sutra puts the limits on the freedom of speech: one should not engage in lying, refrain from impulsiveness, grieve over decline, etc.

Finally, the Sutra also makes a connection with attachment and detachment and grasping; i.e., creating a society that minimizes conflicts and chaos and capable of a different form of governance. In this context, the Sutra ends with a powerful message of the value-base of any system of rights: Not harsh, not greedy, not perturbed, everywhere in tune: this is the reward — I say when asked — for those who are free from pre-conceptions. For one unperturbed — who knows — there's no accumulating. Abstaining, unaroused, he everywhere sees security.

THE VASETÑHA SUTTA

The questions of human rights in this Sutra surfaces out of rather fundamental debate on how a Brahmin is defined in its more comprehensive way. The question was "How do you become a Brahmin?" How a society establishes a social structure among its people. Everything occurs in a dialogue between two young men: Bharadvaja y Vasettha. Bhāradvāja said: *"When you're well born on both your mother's and father's side, of pure descent, with irrefutable and impeccable genealogy back to the seventh paternal generation—then you're a brahmin."* Brahmin out of birth. A birth right. On the other hand Vāseṭṭha was of the opinion that: *"When you're ethical and accomplished in doing your duties—then you're a brahmin".* Brahmin out of actions and deeds, recognized by a society.

They went to the Buddha to hear his opinion. He is extremely clear and explicit. The Buddha uses a taxonomy of species, most of lower nature than human. A summary of the answer given by the Buddha states that grass, trees, quadrupeds, sneak, fish, birds, etc. are defined by birth and as species are indeed diverse. Not by hair, shoulders, head hands, feet, etc. In the case of human they are defined by activity and what they perform daily: farmer, trader, employee, bandit, etc. where the distinctions among human are "spoken by conventions".

In the case of a Brahmin, the Buddha calls a Brahmin someone who has nothing and takes nothing. Someone of sweet words, no clinging, don't steal anything, discarded greed and hate... pure as a spotless moon, knows the passing away and rebirth of all beings, know their past lives... The conclusion is eminently clear: *"You're not a brahmin by birth, nor by birth a non-brahmin. You're a brahmin by your deeds, and by deeds a non-brahmin".*

This is a tremendous theory of human rights. In many of our societies, there are people who exercise power and proclaim wealth out of a birth right and not by rights that surge from actions and deeds. This concept is fundamental as a paradigm in the definition of rights as well as in the exercise any form of rights in our societies. This Sutra demands a profound reflection by all decision-makers in economics, politics and business.

THE ANDHA SUTTA

This is a fascinating Sutra because of the possible multiple interpretations within the context of human rights as well as in other contexts of our societies. To apply the Buddha's teachings here we need to move from "an individual" to "a society", where the same principles advocated in the Sutra apply.

The teachings expressed in the Sutra define a series of pre-conditions to establish a society which is aware and committed to human rights of all beings. There are certain conditions that have defined and determined the character of a society and its capacity to establish and implement rights. We know, that the same rights are understood and implemented differently in different societies. Think about the right of women, children and the right to life.

Herewith a framework to understand rights and responsibilities in different societies.

> **Paraphrasing the Buddha,**
> **there are three kinds of societies in the world:**
> **the blind society,**
> **the one-eyed society**
> **and the two-eyed society.**

First, the blind society does not possess the kind of vision that it is necessary to assign rights and responsibilities.

Second, the one-eyed society have the vision needed to assign rights but does not have the capacity to implement those rights in the proper manner and with the quality needed to do so.

Third, the two-eyed society possesses the vision and the capacity to establish a sound system of rights. It is capable of distinguishing the good and the bad, the competent and the incompetent, and the like.

The same framework could be applied to define the possible systems of justice, its jurisprudence and justiciability of all rights.

In essence, this framework describes one of the most needed pre-conditions to move towards a right-based society.

THE VASALA SUTTA .

In this Sutra, the Budha presents us with various rights, or desirable rights, through the concept of **"Low Life"**. Bharadvaja, treated the Buddha as a person of Low Life. In his response, the Buddha states what he understands by Low Life. I better quote the Sutra:

• "Irritable and hostile, wicked and offensive, a man deficient in view, deceitful: know him as a lowlife.
• He harms living creatures born of womb or of egg, and has no kindness for creatures: know him as a lowlife.
• He destroys and devastates villages and towns, a notorious oppressor: know him as a lowlife.
• Whether in village or wilderness, he steals what belongs to others, taking what has not been given: know him as a lowlife.
• Having fallen into debt, when pressed to pay up he flees, saying 'I don't owe you anything!':know him as a lowlife.
• Wanting some item or other, he attacks a person in the street and takes it: know him as a lowlife.
• For his own sake or the sake of another, or for the sake of wealth, a man tells a lie when asked to bear witness: know him as a lowlife.
• He is spied among the partners Both Norman and Bodhi add a term suggesting transgression here, in line with the commentary and the apparent sense. I don't, as I suspect the text is corrupt. Could diss be duss?of relatives and friends, by force or seduction: know him as a lowlife.
• Though able, he does not look after his mother and father when elderly, past their prime: know him as a lowlife.
• He hits or verbally abuses his mother or father, brother, sister, or mother-in-law: know him as a lowlife.
• When asked about the good, he teaches what is bad, giving secretive advice: know him as a lowlife.
• Having done a bad deed, he wishes, 'May no-one find me out!'His deeds are underhand: know him as a lowlife.
• When visiting another family he eats their delicious food, but does not return the honor: know him as a lowlife.

- He deceives with lies ascetics and brahmins and other nomads: know him as a lowlife.
- When time comes to offer a meal to brahmins or ascetics, he abuses them and does not give: know him as a lowlife.
- He talks about what never happened, being wrapped up in delusion, chasing after some item or other: know him as a lowlife.
- He extols himself and disparages others, brought down by his pride: know him as a lowlife.
- He's a bully and a miser, of corrupt wishes, stingy, and devious, shameless, imprudent: know him as a lowlife.
- He insults the Buddha or his disciple, whether lay or renunciate: know him as a lowlife.
- He claims to be a perfected one, when he really is no such thing. In the world with its Brahmās, that crook is truly the lowest lowlife. These who are called lowlifes I have explained to you.

Chapter 20:

THE RIGHT TO LIFE

(THE DHAMMIKA SUTTA, THE KUTADANTA SUTTA)

"There is no more precious gift you can give than life."

Dr. Pat Robertson

This is a fundamental right and, perhaps, the most important one. The greatest contribution of Buddhism, to a modern form of right to life (sustained in a rather homocentric way), lies on the notion that such a right applies to all possible manifestations of life—i.e., organically including the right of animals and the right to nature. The Buddha repeats this in many of his teachings.

It is worth repeating: for the Buddha, the right to life is a right embedded and applied to all manifestations of life.

In *THE DHAMMIKA SUTTA*, the Buddha teaches Dhammika and the sangha what the life of any householder should look like. Three essential elements of the teaching are clearly stated in that Sutra: (i) a householder should never kill, (ii) nor to create the causes and conditions which would lead up to killing, and (iii) not approve that others may kill. This is a combination of a solid statement on our individual responsibility and teaching about the possible collective consequences of a wrong action. Furthermore, the third requirement shows that for the Buddha it is essential to recognize "collective rights and responsibilities"; i.e., not allow others to harm any form of life. The commandment is neither not to kill someone else, nor to become the source of approval for another person to kill.

Parenthetically, the Universal Declaration of Human Rights (UDHR) explicitly recognizes the right to life as a fundamental right.

The Buddha's teachings on non-violence are also part of the jurisprudence and justiciability of the right to life. An excellent point of departure is **The Five Precepts** *(PANCCA SILA)*; i.e., the essence of the Buddhist path everywhere.

These precepts are commitments: to abstain from killing living beings, stealing, sexual misconduct, lying and intoxication. The practice of these 5 precepts develops many aspects leading finally to our enlightenment.

The presentation from the webpage of "Access to Insight" is extremely useful here:

1. *Panatipata Veramani Sikkhapadam Samadiyami*
I undertake the precept to refrain from destroying living creatures.
2. *Adinnadana Veramani Sikkhapadam Samadiyami*
I undertake the precept to refrain from taking that which is not given.
3. *Kamesu Micchacara Veramani Sikkhapadam Samadiyami*
I undertake the precept to refrain from sexual misconduct.
4. *Musavada Veramani Sikkhapadam Samadiyami*
I undertake the precept to refrain from incorrect speech.
5. *Suramerayamajja Pamadatthana Veramani Sikkhapadam Samadiyami*
I undertake the precept to refrain from intoxicating drinks and drugs which lead to carelessness.

All the above should be complemented with a large number of teachings on avoiding and eliminating violence. The Buddha taught in many ways and forms about the negative impacts of violence. The conclusion is that no one is to engage in any form of violence and that to avoid feeding the cycles of violence (there is a beginning and an end to violence).

Let me now turn to the rights of sentient beings.

There is a tremendously powerful story about the Buddha's view about killing animals and other sentient beings *(THE KUTADANTA SUTTA)*. This is the story of a king who wanted to carry out a sacrifice using cows—i.e., King Mahavijita—Great Dominion. The principal context of this story has to do with the performing sacrifices to the gods. Many of them with the purposes of purification and eliminating bad happenings like crime, theft, and the like. In this case, the proposal was to use 700 animals for such a sacrifice. In the old traditions, the sacrifice for example of horses was believed to strengthen royal authority. But most sacrifices were for lasting welfare and happiness.

The potential impacts of a sacrifice also depended upon the legitimacy of those performing the sacrifice; in this case the high priest and the king. Clearly a legitimacy as perceived by the people in the kingdom. The Buddha explicitly says in the Sutra that "the king governs with the consent of his people". Needless to say, the powerful political statement such words possess.

In our modern societies, not very often one discusses the source of legitimacy of human rights.

In establishing this legitimacy, the Buddha teaches us the important attributes of King Mahavijita: **The Eight Accessories.**

Herewith those accessories:

- *"King Mahavijita possessed eight factors. Royal authority is not based just on birth, conquest, ritual, or power, but on quality of character.*
- *"He was well born on both his mother's and father's side, of pure descent, with irrefutable and impeccable genealogy back to the seventh paternal generation.*
- *"He was attractive, good-looking, lovely, of surpassing beauty. He was magnificent and splendid as Brahmā, remarkable to behold.*
- *"He was rich, affluent, and wealthy, with lots of gold and silver, lots of property and assets, lots of money and grain, and a full treasury and storehouses.*

● *"He was powerful, having an army of four divisions that was obedient and carried out instructions. He'd probably prevail over his enemies just with his reputation. Read sahati ("prevails") over the several variants.*
● *"He was faithful, generous, a donor, his door always open. He was a well-spring of support, making merit with ascetics and brahmins, for paupers, vagrants, nomads, and beggars.*
● *"He was very learned in diverse fields of learning. He understood the meaning of diverse statements, saying: Showing the importance of comprehension over blind adherence to tradition. 'This is what that statement means; that is what this statement means.'*
● *"He was astute, competent, and intelligent, able to think issues through as they bear upon the past, future, and present. Meditators focus on the present, but that does not mean they cannot think about the past or future; it just means they are not trapped in useless thoughts."*

The first one is a fundamental statement, since it recognizes that any person may become enlightened. This is a huge theme that will be address somewhere else (The Buddha and Social Policy). The other ones are relevant attributes of this king, which builds legitimacy to carry out the sacrifice.

The Buddha also listed the accessories of the high priest who was to perform the sacrifice. In essence, the Buddha was establishing the right to perform the sacrifice both by the king and the high priest.

In the end, the sacrifice did not use animals or any other sentient being. The sacrifice did not use trees and, thus. No trees were felled... The sacrifice used other such elements as ghee, oil, butter... This is a tremendous message to all human beings about: (i) how to accomplish an offering or sacrifice and (ii) what are the rights to life of sentient beings and nature.

The Buddha was also asked for forms of sacrifice which may yield great karmic returns. Herewith some examples:

"When someone gives a dwelling specially for the Sangha of the four quarters."
"When someone with confident heart goes for refuge to the Buddha, the teaching, and the Sangha."
"When someone with a confident heart undertakes the training rules to refrain from killing living creatures, stealing, sexual misconduct, lying, and alcoholic drinks that cause negligence."
"The entire path may be described as a "sacrifice".

Chapter 21:

THE RIGHT TO FREE THOUGHT & FREE SPEECH

(THE KALAMA SUTTA)

"This is slavery, not to speak one's thought."

Euripides, The Phoenician Women (5th Century Bc)

Freedom of speech is an essential ingredient of the Universal Declaration of Human Rights. This right, with the rights of thought and related matters have a very important value in our societies and tremendous implications in this era of communications. Within his own society, the Buddha understood this very well. Nobody can be silenced because of their ideas or religion. In fact, all religions today place a major emphasis on this human right. Freedom of expression is presented in many passages and teachings of the Buddha.

THE KALAMA SUTTA has the best and most explicit reference to this issue, expressing the relative importance of the traditional beliefs people had at the time Lord Buddha. The Kalamas complained that many people came to their kingdom to preach their beliefs and religions and, in some cases, demanding the adoption of them. One of the key sentences of the Sutta was that the newcomers were saying their religions were much better than others. The key question for the

Buddha was expressed as follows:

> *"Lord, there are some Brahmans & contemplatives who come
> to Kesaputta. They expound & glorify their own doctrines, but
> as for the doctrines of others, they deprecate them, revile them,
> show contempt for them, & disparage them. And then other
> Brahmans & contemplatives come to Kesaputta. They expound
> & glorify their own doctrines, but as for the doctrines of others,
> they deprecate them, revile them, show contempt for them,
> & disparage them. They leave us absolutely uncertain & in
> doubt: Which of these venerable Brahmans & contemplatives
> are speaking the truth, and which ones are lying?"*

The essence of the teaching is to avoid doubts and act based on your own understanding, and let those rights of expression be respected. The Kalamas had the right to their own beliefs, although it was important that they have a high-quality discriminating mind. The essence of the message is expressed as an important pre-condition of those rights as well as a precondition to having the ability to implement them.

The Buddha making reference to (i) the need to eliminate those doubts and the uncertainty they had respect to their own rights to expression and thought, and (ii) the need to know by themselves what the truth was:

> *"Of course you are uncertain, Kalamas. Of course, you are in
> doubt. When there are reasons for doubt, uncertainty is born.
> So, in this case, Kalamas, don't go by reports, by legends, by
> traditions, by scripture, by logical conjecture, by inference,
> by analogies, by agreement through pondering views, by
> probability, or by the thought, 'This contemplative is our
> teacher.' When you know for yourselves that, 'These qualities
> are unskillful; these qualities are blameworthy; these qualities
> are criticized by the wise; these qualities, when adopted &
> carried out, lead to harm & to suffering' — then you should
> abandon them.*

Without saying whose religion is acceptable or not, the Buddha explicitly gave the blueprint to make such a decision:

> *"Kalamas when you yourself know: These things are bad; these things are blamable; these things are censured by the wise; undertaken and observed, these things lead to harm and ill, abandon them." (Soma Thera 1981: 5-6).*

There is no doubt in my mind that such understanding of rights are fully supported by the essential ingredients in The Noble 8-Fold Path: Right Speech, Right Action and Right Behavior among all others. Thus, The Kalama Sutta may not be looked up in isolation from other teachings. One aspect has to do with the fact that we must not speak falsely; something central to the teachings of the Sutta. A Sutta that is demanding to develop one's critical observation as a precondition of the human right in question.

Venerable Soma Thera's translation of the Sutta brings in a very organized way the elements of that needed critical observation:

1. *Ma Anussavena:*
Do not believe something just because it has been passed along and retold for many generations. [Do not be led by what you are told.]

2. *Ma Paramparaya:*
Do not believe something merely because it has become a traditional practice. [Do not be led by whatever has been handed down from past generations.]

3. *Ma Itikiraya:*
Do not believe something simply because it is well-known everywhere. [Do not be led by hearsay or common opinion.]

4. *Ma Pitakasampadanena:*
Do not believe something just because it is cited in a text. [Do not be led by what the scriptures say.]

5. *Ma Takkahetu:*
Do not believe something solely on the grounds of logical reasoning. [Do not be led by mere logic.]

6. *Ma Nayahetu:*
Do not believe something merely because it accords with your philosophy. [Do not be led by mere deduction or inference.]

7. *Ma Akaraparivitakkena:*
Do not believe something because it appeals to "common sense". [Do not be led by considering only outward appearance.]

8. *Ma Ditthinijjhanakkhantiya:*
Do not believe something just because you like the idea. [Do not be led by preconceived notions (and the theory reflected as an approval)]

9. *Ma Bhabbarupataya:*
Do not believe something because the speaker seems trustworthy. [Do not be led by what seems acceptable; do not be led by what seemingly believable person says.]

10. *Ma Samano No Garuti:*
Do not believe something thinking, *"This is what our teacher says"*. [Do not be led by what your teacher tells you] _ (Kinnes, 1995, p. 6)

The above list is also known as **"The Buddha's Charter of Free Inquiry"**

Chapter 22:

THE BUDDHA & HUMAN POVERTYH

(THE INA SUTTA, THE CAKKAVATTI SIHANANDA SUTTA, THE KUTADANTA SUTTA, THE RATHAPALLA SUTTA)

"Poverty is the worst form of violence"

Mahatma Gandhi

There is no doubt that economics, development and poverty play a significant role in the Buddha's teachings. Part of the power of those teachings has to do with the social situation and the implications in daily life. At the center stage was the notion and the implications of material wealth in our spiritual path towards enlightenment. At the time, it was imperative to improve people's lives and welfare, and the Buddha did not want to separate spirituality from economics and politics.

This approach was nurtured by the mutual interaction needed between the creation and acquisition of wealth and the ethics of doing so. For the Buddha, these two were inseparable. Specifically, neither politics nor economics could be exercised within an ethics vacuum.

One of the important contexts of economics had to do with socio institutional degradation, translated into human poverty. The Buddha recognized this in a series of teachings, which may become useful today, in private and public decision-making, and to create new narratives for the traditional notions of welfare economics. A welfare economics with moral and ethical foundations.

Some of the passages have already been cited in previous sections of this Part of the Book, under the rubric of "wealth". One example is that of the Andha Sutta, in which there is a detailed explanation of the relationship between wealth and the ethics of acqu iring and spending wealth accumulated (the blind, one-eyed and the two-eyed persons).

In most situations, poverty was an outcome of that process of wealth creation, and other personal and collective considerations (right livelihood, right effort and right action).

In *THE INA SUTTA*, the Buddha presents poverty as a major source of suffering. Specifically, the Sutta states:

> *"So mendicants, poverty, debt, interest, warnings, prosecution, and imprisonment are suffering in the world for those who enjoy sensual pleasures. In the same way, whoever has no faith, conscience, prudence, energy, and wisdom when it comes to skillful qualities is called poor and penniless in the training of the Noble One."*
>
> *"Since they have no faith, conscience, prudence, energy, or wisdom when it comes to skillful qualities, they do bad things by way of body, speech, and mind. This is how they're in debt, I say."*
>
> *"In order to conceal the bad things they do by way of body, speech, and mind they harbour corrupt wishes. They wish, plan, speak, and act with the thought: 'May no-one find me out!' This is how they pay interest, I say."*
>
> *"...Poverty is said to be suffering in the world, and so is being in debt. A poor person who has fallen into debt frets even when spending the loan..."(Iṇasutta—Bhikkhu Sujato, Numbered Discourses 6. "Debt".)*

As it is observed here, the Buddha presents a very comprehensive description of the situation, including other such dimensions as debt.

Furthermore, in other texts referred to earlier, the suffering comes from not being able to function in the society and to be able to satisfy the basic needs, as well as being incapacitated to make offerings (to do merits). The bottom line here is the advancement in the material and the spiritual are highly correlated. A sable society must be materially and spiritually reach.

In one instance, the Buddha did not begin teaching a very hungry person. He fed him first and, then, he imparted the teachings.

THE CAKKAVATTI SIHANANDA SUTTA contains many passages describing several causes and conditions of poverty. The first and principal one had to do with a change in the style of governance between the king and his crown prince. The latter adopted its own ways and, as a result, society became poorer and social instability increased.

The Sutra is a very detailed in the way it describes the cycles of poverty and instability. Actually, the Sutra shows how collective social behavior may change as a result of one mistake in decision making—e.g., benefiting one thief who argued that he was a thief out of poverty. There is a comprehensive description of how a society may easily decline in collective welfare.

There was a real need to do merits in order to change the downturn direction of society. Herewith a description of the critical importance of merits:

> *"And then the thought will occur to those beings: "It is only because we became addicted to evil ways that we suffered this loss of our kindred, so let us now do good! What good things can we do? Let us abstain from the taking of life - that will be a good practice." And so they will abstain from the taking of life, and, having undertaken this good thing, will practise it. And through having undertaken such wholesome things, they*

> *will increase in life-span and beauty. And the children of those whose life-span was ten years will live for twenty years.*
>
> *'Then it will occur to those beings: "It is through having taken to wholesome practices that we have increased in life-span and beauty, so let us perform still more wholesome practices. Let us refrain from taking what is not given, from sexual misconduct, from lying speech, from slander, from harsh speech, from idle chatter, from covetousness, from ill-will, from wrong views; let us abstain from three things: incest, excessive greed, and deviant practices; let us respect our mothers and fathers, ascetics and Brahmins, and the head of the clan, and let us persevere in these wholesome actions."*
>
> *"And so they will do these things, and on account of this they will increase in life-span and in beauty..."*

In many teachings, the Buddha suggest what should a ruler do to take people out of poverty. One example is given in *THE KUTADANTA SUTTA*, which we have cited in this book a few times. The emphasis here is on the importance of food for the people and fodder for the animals; two very important basic needs.

The policy prescription is that the government has to contribute to each human activity in some ways to come out of poverty, and ensure economic progress. The policy prescription is not just to increase taxes and pubic revenues from the people.

Poverty also limits the poor to do offerings and to practice such virtues as generosity, in order to accumulate merits. A very important linkage between the type of material society we have and the ability to attain enlightenment via the practice of merits.

Finally, I would like to refer to a very comprehensive Sutra, which teaches us a large number of subject matters.

This is *THE RATHAPALLA SUTTA*. The beautiful life of Venerable Rathapalla, who had some difficulties to become a monk, as his parents did not want to give permission to him. However, after having that parental permission, Rathapalla became an Arhant, and his teachings were really elightening. Here with some passages to deeply reflect upon (from Thanissaru Bikkhu version):

In this Sutra, there is a fundamental concept, extremely applicable to the situation today: **we do not own the world.** And, when we think we do, we are on very shaky grounds. At one point, Rathapalla states:

> "It was in reference to this, great king, that the Blessed One who knows & sees, worthy & rightly self-awakened, said: 'The world is without ownership. One has to pass on, leaving everything behind.' Having known & seen & heard this, I went forth from the home life into homelessness.
>
> "It was in reference to this, great king, that the Blessed One who knows & sees, worthy & rightly self-awakened, said: 'The world is insufficient, insatiable, a slave to craving.' Having known & seen & heard this, I went forth from the home life into homelessness."

The above is expanded with poetry at the end of the Sutra:

> "I see in the world
> people with wealth
> who, from delusion,
> don't make a gift
> of the treasure they've gained.
> Greedy, they stash it away,
> hoping for even more
> sensual pleasures.
>
> Long life
> can't be gotten with wealth,
> nor aging
> warded off with treasure.

> *The wise say this life*
> *is next to nothing —*
> *impermanent, subject to change.*
>
> *Thus, the discernment by which*
> *one attains to mastery,*
> *is better than wealth —*
> *for those who haven't reached mastery*
> *go from existence to existence,*
> *out of delusion,*
> *doing bad deeds."*

This Sutra insists on something we have been hammering everywhere in this book: material wealth is not all, and it must be accompanied with a social doctrine of ethic and morals. Otherwise, wealth creation does more harm than good.

This is specifically stated when Rathapalla says: *"the discernment by which one attains to mastery, is better than (material--added) wealth"*. In other words, **wealth creation and mastery go together; i.e., they are inseparable.**

That applies to any level of wealth, to the rich and the poor. To a rich nation or a poor nation. Mastery is an indispensable part of an individual or collective strategy. Today's capitalist system is materially rich but spiritually poor: very minimal mastery or very little ethics and moral.

Part

3

A Personal
Letter To You

THE EPILOGUE

"A call for humanity: Restoring our moral compass"

This book was completed when most planetary citizens were preparing for a possible World War III. Riots in many cities and communities, discontent with the state of play, massive migration as a result of instability and ecological destruction, fear about a very fragile future, aggressive religious persecutions, progressive violations of basic rights, and absolute poverty and marginalization everywhere, are signaling the desperate situation facing billions of people. Also, the presence of war between Russia and Ukraine, Israel and Palestine, and more, coupled with a huge weakening of democratic and participatory institutions, nationally and globally. Not less important, our common public goods are managed by an outdated Multilateral System incapable of reaching any reasonable lasting solutions or consensus about our common destiny.

Most probably than not, a worldwide conflict will be a nuclear war of major consequences: the total devastation of the planet. It is difficult to imagine the physical and psychological consequences of such a nuclear war.

At this moment in history, technology advances faster than wisdom, and material power is often mistaken for virtue. The world not only faces a political, economic, business, and environmental crisis, but also a crisis of conscience and ethics.

We witness the rapid erosion of our moral foundations and, as a result, it is more complex to hold our planetary civilization together. Thus, the truth is no longer sacred, integrity has become negotiable, compassion is treated as weakness, and justice is too often dismissed as optional or inconvenient. It is not that we do not know what is right; we have learned how to look away.

We are told that these are the costs of modern economic and social development, that morality should be kept as something personal, and that ethics is something subjective. That we cannot afford to care for other human beings, sentient beings, and nature.

> **Today, the children grow up in war zones and are crying from hunger and desperation**

This is a suicidal path for humanity. History demonstrates that without a shared moral ground, we cannot stand together as a civilization. Simply, without a developed 'collective consciousness', there can be no civilization at all.

Today, the children grow up in war zones and are crying by hunger and desperation while the world debates politics; the earth itself cries out in droughts, floods, and fires, and we continue to consume without thought; the families are being ripped apart and communities are being dismantled culturally, socially, and value-wise; and the vulnerable are silenced, the powerful are protected, and the rest of us are taught to keep our heads down. What has happened to our humanity?

As a child, my soul was opened to address a major question: **Why have I been born at this juncture of human history?** Born at a moment of great transition, major transformations, fuller awareness, and boundaryless states of reality. Soon after this question surfaced, I realized that I could not escape from seeing, understanding, and self-realizing all there is to experience in life: the good, the bad, and the ugly. It was not only about understanding and self-realizing the 'good', but also experiencing life in all its expressions. A tremendously rich reincarnation.

We are living in an age where **"moral courage and empowerment"** have become rare, and ethical compromise is said to be the price of success. Where truth and facts are often twisted for short-term gains, and human lives are weighed against convenience or political returns.

We must ask ourselves: what kind of world are we building for the youth and future generations when we no longer ask what is right but only what is materially useful?

This is the year 2025, when my physical body became 78 years old. I have lived on this planet for almost eight decades of impressive material progress: from communicating by written letters—with pencil and paper--that were delivered several months later, by ships, trains, bullock carts or horses, to the era of supersonic airplanes, fast-speed trains, spaceships, satellites, laptops, cellular phones, and instant communications by the abilities of social media. I have lived in communities, villages, small cities, and mega urban spaces, crowded, noisy, and contaminated.

Today, we witness various forms of violence and conflict in every corner. In most societies, there is some form of fragmentation, separation, or duality, which forces most people to live on extremes of the socio-political spectrum. This is expressed through narratives of all sorts: left and right, east and west, north and south, developed and underdeveloped, capitalist and communist, rich and poor, white and black... These are a major source of tension and extremism, significantly eroding whatever efforts have been made or are being made to reach collective harmony and peace.

> **Today, we witness various forms of violence and conflict in every corner.**

The materialistic dream of 'having', 'possessing', and 'accumulating' more and more is slowly vanishing. History has proven that having more is not tantamount to being more. "Materiality Only" as the collective path to humanity neither resolves our material problems any longer, nor our challenges embedded in spiritual transformation.

It is evident that despite all the material progress we see today, there are millions of people left behind. Despite all we may say about our contributions to some 'common good', we witness how rapidly biodiversity is being depleted, how most sources of fresh water are being polluted, and how billions of people are suffering deeply from climate change and global warming. Despite all the advances and attainments of human collective consciousness, we are not yet able to self-realize what may be referred to as 'The Two Hundred Society': a society that is both materially and spiritually rich, at the same time. From almost every angle, I see that we are embracing societies that are materially rich but spiritually poor.

The Social Doctrines that have been supporting and nurturing this materialistic system have failed us, and A New Social Doctrine has to emerge the soonest.

Today, we live a life where 'Material Individualism' dominates all aspects of our societies. We can experience the power of communication technologies that allow us to see each other right now, instantly, without any boundaries, and to experience your existence, over space and time. We live a life where time has been reduced to almost zero in many situations.

Today, the destruction of our outer ecology is immense, and it is not known with certainty whether we have passed the point of no return. I have no doubts that the destruction of the outer ecology is correlated with the state of our inner ecology: our inner being, our refined mind, and our level of consciousness. Thus, it will not be possible to resolve the issues we experience in our outer world without a major transformation of our inner selves. In doing so, and perhaps as a precondition to all we may do in the future, it is fundamental to reconcile spirituality with economics, politics, governance, and social institutions. Not a trivial task, as it demands to eliminate the Duality between the Having and the Being.

We must acknowledge that life is also a collection of miracles and a bountiful expression of existence. But we do not stop and think of it. Since I was born, my mind and soul have hinted to me that this Earth is our true Heaven, not as a matter of faith, but as a reality I had to self-realize deeply in my heart. I know and experience daily the tremendous privilege to have been born here on Earth. Accordingly, I am also fully aware that this privilege entails many individual and collective responsibilities; one of those collective and shared responsibilities is to protect Creation. Not an insignificant reality.

> **The problems we face today have not dropped from thin air**

More often than not, we just want more and more material things without any limits (greed). It is a fact that various social, business, and political actors develop and engage within a tremendous ethical and moral vacuum.

The problems we face today have not dropped from thin air. They result from the accumulation of past actions and their corresponding consequences. Your actions, my actions, our collective actions. Simply said, we are the fruit of our karma, individual and collective karma. Suffering is a fruit of our karma. Fear is a fruit of our karma. Uncertainty is a fruit of our karma.

To change the course of humanity demands a drastic rudder stroke regarding our habits, behaviors, decisions, and actions, to name a few. These will, in turn, change our vision, intent, action, behavior, and efforts.

There is too much unnecessary individual and social suffering in the world. The material solutions that have been offered to date have not been capable of resolving the existing problems facing humanity any longer. Therefore, we must make all our efforts to find new and effective solutions capable of eliminating individual and social suffering, no matter where this suffering comes from.

In this book, I have shared with you what I believe are the fundamental attributes and ingredients of effective and lasting solutions for humanity's challenges, issues, and problems. I called them 'The Buddhist Solutions' as they ought to embody important inner transformations (starting with our inner ecology), where our inner development becomes the fundamental ingredient.

As human beings, we will not be able to find solutions beyond what our consciousness allows us to find. Our constraint is not 'technology', understood in a traditional sense. What truly matters for humanity today is the level of individual and collective consciousness. The corresponding spiritual law is that at every moment we are bound by our capacity to transcend and our abilities to Be, to Inter-Be, to Inter-We, and to Become. The lesson is that **'we are not aware that we are not aware'.** It is through consciousness raising that we break that cycle of awareness.

I call on the entire humanity to seriously consider a rather unique spiritual path. Please, this is not as if you would need to adopt a new religion. I do not mean that: keep your own religion and faith. My proposal is not a call for some form of 'religious conversion'. In fact, this is a call to know, understand, and consider the path of love, compassion, equanimity, trust, justice, respect... that I have shared with you in this book. This call must not be difficult to embrace by all major religions of the world. The Book's emphasis and foundations are 'The Social Teachings' of the Buddha. And, based on those social teachings, construct 'A Social Doctrine' to guide humanity's present and future, in a world now dominated by 'Individual Materialism'. As you have seen in Part II, the Book offers some practical reviews and examples related to foundational ideas and instruments for A New Social Doctrine for humanity. I will not repeat them here.

The time has come to awaken our wisdom and compassion and the entire collective conscience; to join hands for a better future despite our differences; to promote and self-realize inner and outer peace; to commit ourselves to the construction of a compassionate society; and to remind people of commonly shared responsibilities and spiritual values.

Human dignity means that every human being, sentient being, and nature has inherent worth regardless of such secondary identities like race, gender, nationality, wealth, religion, or social status. Human dignity must emphasize the sacredness of life everywhere and in all its manifestations, and thus, nobody can be dehumanized or neglected.

Our societies and the world at large have become fragmented, and we must stop it. We know that we are different in cultures, ethnicity, religions, politics.... But these differences should not stop us from having shared goals, rights, and responsibilities, because we have a common destiny. This is the only way to attain peace, justice, security, cooperation....

It is imperative to have the moral courage to speak up and act when facing injustice and inequality. An empowered future must be established; this demands a new vision and commitment to a world that embraces some core fairness for all. This is not about giving charity but a powerful moral imperative. The dignity of all manifestations of life is not conditional. Thus, we must choose to see each other not as enemies, strangers, or statistics but as one united community of beings.

The book has offered a new vision. Within this context, global solidarity and caring for creation are fundamental pillars. Thus, we have to work through hope and renewal, despite the fragmentation we witness today. We have a collective shared future, and thus, it is necessary to engage in joint efforts now.

Let our wisdom and compassion rise higher than our fears. Let us stop corruption in leadership and institutions. Let us eliminate injustice within legal systems and not allow unnecessary inequality and exploitation. Let us not accept the atomization of people for profit or power. Let us not be indifferent to suffering. Let our merits and actions eliminate the erosion of truth, integrity, and accountability. Let us not normalize violence or dishonesty. Let us not close our eyes to the exploitation of the poor and vulnerable, as profit is prioritized over people. Let our hearts and souls stop environmental degradation driven by greed. Let our wisdom intervene in technologies being used unethically.

We, together, must avoid at all costs The Ethical Collapse of our planetary society. Ethics is not an elite philosophy. Ethics is the architecture of empathy, compassion, responsibility, and justice. It is Ethics that will guide us to construct a new future. Let this be the moment we reclaim our moral compass.

We already know that when Ethics is treated as optional, humanity suffers. We must not let trust die. We must not create a vacuum of justice and peace. We must self-realize compassion so that our civilization does not continue becoming like another machine. We are not meant to be machines. We are meant to be human beings.

Each of us has a voice, a choice, and a responsibility.

Thus, humanity must not be measured by its power or material wealth, but by its capacity to establish a form of livelihood that is just, truthful, compassionate, and responsible. Remember that 'morality lives in the choices we make.'

We must rebuild the world on the foundation of A New Social Doctrine. One that makes clear that material success without conscience soon becomes a failure.

Let us hold our leaders accountable not by their promises, but by their self-realization of human and spiritual values. A just, compassionate, peaceful, and equitable world will be born from millions of small, moral acts of resistance and love.

We may speak different languages, pray in different ways, live under different flags, but **we belong to one planetary civilization**. What we choose to ignore today will return to us tomorrow.

Future generations will not judge us by the millions of buildings and highways we constructed, but by who we became as a planetary society.

We still have time. But not forever. Let us choose to become enlightened humans, together.

"I am because you are, and you are because I am."

In service to humanity,

Dzambling Cho Tab Khen

(Alfredo Sfeir Younis)

Part

4

A Buddhist Social Doctrine:
THE IMPERATIVE OF
EDUCATION AND TRAINING

Annex 1:

SOME SALIENT BOOKS TO CONSIDER

The concept of a "Planetary Vinaya" may not be explicitly covered in traditional Buddhist texts, as it is a contemporary interpretation that combines Buddhist principles with environmental sustainability. However, there are several modern texts and books that address the connection between Buddhism and ecology, and which could provide insight into a Buddhist-inspired approach to sustainable living. Some of these include:

1. "The World We Have:

A Buddhist Approach to Peace and Ecology" by Thich Nhat Hanh - This book explores the connection between Buddhist practice and environmental sustainability.

2. "Buddhism and Ecology: The Interconnection of Dharma and Deeds"

Edited by Mary Evelyn Tucker and Duncan Ryuken Williams - This book presents essays by various experts on the relationship between Buddhism and the ecology.

3. *"Ecology and the End of Postmodernity"*

By George Handley - This book examines how spirituality and ecology can work together to address current environmental challenges.

4. *"Green Buddhism: Practice and Compassionate Action in Uncertain Times"*

By Stephanie Kaza - This book explores how Buddhist practice can inform our actions to address the environmental crisis.

These books can provide a broader perspective on how Buddhist principles can be applied to environmental sustainability and creating a more conscious and planet-friendly lifestyle.

Annex 2:

LIST OF READINGS

· "Una Aproximación al Budismo"
Antonio Minguez Reguera. Federación de Comunidades Budistas de España (FCBE).

· "Principles of Catholic Social Teachings"
Micah Institute for Business and Economics. Seton Hall University.

· "The Buddha's Teachings on Social and Communal Harmony: An Anthology of Discourses from the Pali Canon".
The Teachings of the Buddha. Amazon. December 13, 2016.

· "Consciousness, Collective Consciousness Enlightenment and Collective Enlightenment". Allan Combs.

· "Collective Enlightenment".
George Por, Sahlan Momo, and Roger Nelson. Spanda Journal, VII (1). 2017.

· "Is Buddhist Enlightenment Evolving to Become More Communal".
In: Is Individual Spirituality Expanding? September 30, 2016.

· "Ashoka The Visionary", by Ashoka Khanna, World Bank. 1818 Society. March 1, 2024.

· "Ashokan Inscriptions." TestBook.Com. April 17, 2023.

· "Major Rocks of Ashoka". Wikipedia,
https://en.wikipedia.org/wiki/Major_Rock_Edicts#Major_Rock_Edict_

· "Ashoka and The Decline of the Mauryas". Romila Thapar. Revised Edition. Oxford University Press. 1997. Appendix V: A Translation of the Edicts of Ashoka.

· "Ashoka the Great: India's Mauryan Emperor".
National Geographic

· "The Legacy of King Ashoka".
Live History India

· "Ashoka: The Great Emperor". Ancient History Encyclopedia

· "Edicts of Ashoka".
Britannica

· "Buddhist Policies of King Ashoka".
JSTOR

· "Ashoka the Great: The King and the Man".
Upinder Singh

· "Ashoka: The Search for India's Lost Emperor".
Charles Allen

· "Ashoka: The World's First Emperor".
Nayanjot Lahiri

· "Ashoka: The Buddhist Emperor of India".
Vincent A. Smith

· "Ashoka in Ancient India".
Nirmala Rao

· "Ashoka's Administration and Economy".
Amruta Patil. 2024.

· "Buddhist Economics".
Wikipedia,

· "King Asoka as a Role Model of Buddhist Leadership".
Thomas Voss.

· "To Uphold the World: The Economic Thought of Ashoka and Kautilya".
Bruce Rich, J.D. September 14, 2018.

· "Top 40+Gautam Buddha Quotes for Inspiration and Motivation".
Jagran Josh. TWINKLE. May 22, 2024.

· "Devadatta—Greatest Enemy of the Buddha".
Peter Vredeveld. Original Buddhas Webpage. Undated.

· "Defining Lesser and Minor Rules".
Bhante Sujato. Sutta Central. March 2023.

· "Conscious Sustainability Leadership: A New Paradigm For Next Generation Leaders". Alfredo Sfeir-Younis and Marco Tavanti . (SDG Series) Paperback – May 17, 2020.

· "The Buddha's Strategies for Happiness : II".
Thanissaro Bhikku. Dharma Talks. 2013.

· "The Impact of Buddhism on Chinese Culture".
John Kieschnick, 2003.

· "Essential Elements of Human Rights in Buddhism".
Uttamkumar S. Bagde. Applied Microbiology Laboratory, Department of Life Sciences, University of Mumbai, Vidyanagari, Santacruz (East) Mumbai- 4000098, India. May 2014.

· "Buddhism and Human Rights".
Saneh Chamarik. Faculty of Political Science Thammasat University Bangkok. (Preamble by Phra Raja- varamuni Payutto. Thai Khadi Research Institute Thammasat University Bangkok, Thailand 1982.

· "Buddhism and Human Rights: Gotama Buddha's Contributions to the Development of Human Rights".
Khem Bun. Paññasastra University of Cambodia, PUC. Phnom Penh, Cambodia.

· "Buddhists and Human Rights".
Robert Traer. Revision of Material in Faith in Human Rights: Support in Religious Traditions for a Global Struggle (Washington, DC: Georgetown University Press, 1991).

· "Are There 'Human Rights' in Buddhism?".
Damien Keown. University of London, Goldsmiths. Damine V. Keown, Charles S. Prebish, and Wayne R. Husted, edited. Curzon Press. 1998, pp. 239.

· "Non-Violence: A Study Guide".
Thanissaro Bhikkhu. Access to Insight (BCBS Edition. 30 November 2013. http://www.accesstoinsight.org/lib/study/nonviolence.html .

· "Introduction to the Patimokkha Rules". Thanissaro
Bhikkhu. Access to Insight (BCBS Edition), 17 December 2013. http://www.accesstoinsight.org/tipitaka/vin/sv/bhikkhu-pati-intro.html

· "Universal Declaration of Human Rights and the Buddhist Teaching".
Unuwaturabubule Mahinda Thero. Social Sciences and Humanities Review, Volume 02, No. 02, March 2015, ISSN: 2279-3933.

· "Articulating Human Rights in the Context of Buddhist Ethics in Sri Lanka".
FOCUS. September 1997 Volume 9.

· "The Buddhist Perspective of Life and the Idea of Human Rights".
Yoichi Kawada. Journal of Oriental Studies 30–1: 110.

· "The World We Have: A Buddhist Approach to Peace and Ecology".
Thich Nhat Hanh.

· "Buddhism and Ecology: The Interconnection of Dharma and Deeds".
Mary Evelyn Tucker and Duncan Ryuken Williams (eds.).

· "Ecology and the End of Postmodernity".
George Handley.

· "Green Buddhism: Practice and Compassionate Action in Uncertain Times".
Stephanie Kaza.

· "The Social Dimensions of Early Buddhism".
Chakravarti, U. New Delhi: Oxford University Press, 1987.

· "Being Benevolence: The Social Ethics of Engaged Buddhism".
Sallie B. King. University of Hawaii Press, Honolulu, 2005.

· "Engaged Buddhism: Buddhist Liberation Movements in Asia".
Christopher S. Queen and Sallie B. King. State of New York University Press,
Albany, 1996.

· "Becoming Socially Engaged in Burma: The Utilization of Buddhism in the
Protection of Human Rights"
Leslie Reilly

· "Being Peace".
Thich Nhat Hanh.

· "Ethics for a New Millennium".
H.H. The Dalai Lama.

· "The Engaged Buddhist Reader".
Arnold Kotler.

· "Engaged Buddhism in the West".
Christopher Queen.

· "Hooked".
Stephanie Kaza.

· "What the Buddha Taught".
Walpola Rahula.

· "The Heart of the Buddha's Teaching".
Thich Nhat Hanh.

· "The Middle Length Discourses of the Buddha: A New Translation of the
Majjhima Nikaya". Nanamoli, Bhikkhu and Bhikkhu Bodhi, trans. Boston:
Wisdom, 1995.

· "Inner Revolution: Life, Liberty, and the Pursuit of Real Happiness".
Robert Thurman

· "The Holy Teaching of Vimalakirti: A Mahayana Scripture".
Thurman, Robert A. F., trans. University Park, Pa.: Pennsylvania State University Press, 1976.

· "The Way of the Bodhisattva: A Translation of the Bodhicharyavatara".
Shantideva. New York: Random House, 1997.

· "Being Benevolence: The Social Ethics of Engaged Buddhism".
Sallie B. King. University of Hawaii Press, Honolulu, 2005.

· "The Universal Declaration of Human Rights".
United Nations. http://www.un.org/en/ documents/udhr, 2012.

· "Engaged Buddhism in the West".
Christopher S. Queen. Wisdom Publications, Boston, 2000.

The Sutras

• THE CUNDA KAMMARAPUTTA SUTTA, in a dialogue between the Buddha and a silversmith called Cunda (see the translation from Pali carried out by Thanissaro Bhikkhu. 1997);

• THE AMBALATTHIKA RAHULOVADA SUTTA, in a dialogue with Buddha's son Rahula (see the translation by Thannissaro Bhikkhu. 2006);

• THE VATTHUPAMA SUTTA: The Smile of the Cloth
(see the translation by Nyanaponika Thera. 1998);

• THE MAHA-CATTARISAKA SUTTA: The Great Forty
(see translation by Thanissaro Bhikkhu. 2008);

• THE SAMMADITTHI SUTTA: The Discourse on the Right View (see translation by Thanissaro Bhikkhu and Ñanamoli Thera with Bhikkhu Bodhi. 1998);

• THE (AKUSALA) KAMMA NIDANA SUTTA: Causes of Karma
(see translation by Piya Tan. 2007);

• THE DUCCARITAVIPAKA SUTTA
(see translation of Sutta Central, with Thanissaro Bhikkhu).

• THE ADIYA SUTTA: Benefits to be Obtained from Wealth
(see translation by Thanissaro Bhikkhu. 1997). And,

• THE ANATHPINDIKOVADA SUTTA: Instructions to Anathapindika (see translation by Thanissaro Bhikkhu. 2003).

• THE DAMMIKA SUTTA: Dhammika (see translation by John D. Ireland. 1994).

• THE METTA SUTTA: Discourse on Unconditional Love (In Spanish, by Grego Davila. 5 April 2012. Publish in Blog Sabiduria. Grego.ES)

• THE KALAMA SUTTA: The Buddha's Charter of Free Inquiry
(See translation by Soma Thera. 1994).

• THE DHAMMACAKKAPPAVATTANA SUTTA: Setting the Wheel of Dhamma in Motion (See translation by Thanissaro Bhikkhu. 1993).

• THE VASETTHA SUTTA: With Vasettha.
(See translation by Bhikkhu Sujato).

• THE AMBATTHA SUTTA: With Ambattha.
(See translaton by Bhikkhu Sujato).

• THE MADHUPINDIKA SUTTA: The Ball of Honey.
(See Translation by Thanissaro Bhikkhu. 1999.).

• THE TEVIJJA SUTTA: The Experts in The Three Vedas.
(See translation by Bhikkhu Sujato).

• THE BRAMHAJĀLA SUTTA: The All-Embracing Net of Views.
(See translation by Bhikkhu Bodhi. 2010.).

• THE KALAHAVIVĀDA SUTTA: Quarrels and Disputes.
(See translation by Thanissaro Bhikkhu. 1994.).

• THE ATTADANDA SUTTA: The Rod Embraced.
(See translation by Thanissaro Bhikkhu. 1995.).

• THE ESUKĀRI SUTTA: With Esukari.
(See translation by Bhikkhu Sujato).

• THE AGGAÑA SUTTA: What Came First.
(See translation of Bhikkhu Sujato).

• THE MAHA-RAHULOVĀD SUTTA: The Great Exhortation to Rahula.
(See translation by Thanissaro Bhikkhu. 2006).

• THE SIGALOVADA SUTTA: The Discourse to Sigala.
(See translation by Narada Thera. 1996.).

• THE CAKKAVATTI-SIHANANDA SUTTA: The Wheel Turning Emperor (See translation by Thanissaro Bhikkhu. 2002).

• THE KUTADANTA SUTTA: With Kutadanta—The People From The Brahmanic Cast of Khanumata (See translation by Anton P. Baron).

• THE NIPATA SUTTA: The Sutta Collection
(See compilation by Thanissaro Bhikkhu. 2005.).

• THE VASALA SUTTA: Discourse on Outcasts.
(See translation by Piyadassi Thera. 1999.).

• THE KANNAKATTHALA SUTTA: At Kannakatthala
(See translation by Thanissaro Bhikkhu. 2003).

• THE KARANIYA METTA SUTTA: The Buddha's Words on Loving-Kindness (See translation by The Amaravati Sangha. 2004).

• THE VANAROPA SUTTA: Planters
(See translation by Bhikkhu Sujato).

• THE MAHA MANGALA SUTTA: Blessings
(See translation by Narada Thera. 1994).

• THE MAHA-PARINIBBANA SUTTA: Last Days of the Buddha (See translation by Sister Vajira & Francis Story. 1998).

• THE VIBHANGA SUTTA: Analysis of The Feeling Faculties (See translation by Thanissaro Bhikkhu. 2005).

• THE MAHACATTARISAKA SUTTA: The Great Forty (See translation by Thanissaro Bhikkhu. 2008).

• THE CHANNOVADA SUTTA: Advice to Channa.
(See translation of Bhikkhu Sujato).

• THE CUNDA KAMMARAPUTTA SUTTA: To Cunda The Silversmith.
(See translation of Thanissaro Bhikkhu. 1997).

• THE VAKKALI SUTTA: Vakkali.
(See the translation by Maurice O'Connell Walsh. 2007.)

• THE GODHIKA SUTTA: Godhi.
(See the translation of Bhikkhu Bodhi).

• THE ADITTAPARIYAYA SUTTA: The Fire Sermon.
(See the translation by Thanissaro Bhikkhu. 1993.).

• THE SARABHA SUTTA: Sarabha.
(See the translation by Bhikkhu Bodhi).

• THE LATUKIKOPAMA SUTTA: The Quail Simile.
(See the translation by Thanissaro Bhikkhu. 2003.)

SUTTACENTRAL
https://suttacentral.net › sujato

ACCESS TO INSIGHT
https://www.accesstoinsight.org › ...

Copyrights Pictures

• Page 106: "Buddha Statue"
https://www.freepik.com/premium-photo/peaceful-statue-buddha_253666236.htm

• Page 111: "Young Students Monks"
https://www.freepik.es/fotos-premium/grupo-monjes-estan-pie-frente-edificio_210238337.htm

• Page 112: " "Manuscript"
https://wellcomecollection.org/works/waf43t78 CC-BY-4.0

• Page 116: " King Suddhodana and Queen Mahamaya (28682062671).jpg"
https://commons.wikimedia.org/wiki/File:008c_KIng_Suddhodana_and_Queen_Mahamaya_(28682062671).jpg

• Page 120: "Buddha's golden Statues"
https://www.freepik.com/free-photo/buddha-statue_1030807.htm

• Page 132: "Buddha Statue Zoom"
https://www.freepik.es/fotos-premium/estatua-budas_17394888.htm

• Page 138: "Buddha, Wat Maha That"
https://www.freepik.es/foto-gratis/cabeza-buda-higuera-wat-maha-that-parque-historico- ayutthaya-tailandia_13180828.htm#from_view=detail_alsolike

• Page 142: "Monk with an elephant"
https://www.gettyimages.es/detail/foto/monk-and-elephant-at-surin-province-thailand-imagen-libre-de-derechos/937645626

• Page 147: "Scene from the Life of the Buddha", Japanese painting, early 15th century.
https://www.metmuseum.org/art/collection/search/45212

• Page 148: "Tibet mountains"
https://www.freepik.es/imagen-ia-premium/templo-tibet-cima-montana-edificio-arquitectura- punto-referencia_256036048.htm

• Page 155: "Buddha Ngong Ping, Hong Kong"
https://www.freepik.es/fotos-premium/estatua-buda-gigante-ngong-ping-hong-kong_8174282.htm

• Page 156: "Monks in the Temple"
https://idn.freepik.com/foto-premium/tampak-belakang-para-biksu-berdiri-di-depan-dinding_100074027.htm

• Page 162: "Animal Sacrificed"
https://upload.wikimedia.org/wikipedia/commons/9/90/Sacrifice_boar_Louvre_G112.jpg

• Page 164: "Floating-pagoda-temple-chae-hom-district-lam-pang-thailand"
https://www.freepik.es/foto-gratis/pagoda-flotante-pico-montana-templo-wat-chaloem-phra-kiat-phra-bat-pupha-daeng-distrito-chae-hom-lampang-tailandia_26330471.htm

• Page 174: "Novices meditating"
https://www.freepik.es/fotos-premium/novatos-estan-meditando-sitios-antiguos_3830393.htm

• Page 190: "A Buddha statue with the sun behind it"
https://www.freepik.com/premium-photo/statue-face-with-sun-it_216811733.htm

• Page 195: "Monks walking"
https://www.freepik.es/fotos-premium/seccion-baja-personas-que-us-an-ropa-tradicional-naranja-mientras-caminan-carretera_96462433.htm#-from_element=cross_selling___photo&position=6

• Page 196: "Geometric Thangka"
https://es.wikipedia.org/wiki/Archivo:Chakrasamvara_Mandala.jpg

• Page 207: "Tantric Form of the Bodhisattva Manjushri"
https://www.meisterdrucke.es/impresion-art%C3%ADstica/Unbekan-nt/1203280/Mandala-de-las-formas-de-Manjushri,-el-Bodhisattva-de-la-Sabidur%C3%ADa-Trascendente,-finales-del-siglo-XIV.html

• Page 208: "A young monk from Myanmar"
https://www.shutterstock.com/es/image-photo/southeast-asian-myanmar-little-monk-reading-153016409

• Page 210: "Students"
https://www.freepik.es/fotos-premium/monjes-leyendo-libro-mientras-caminan-pasillo_96409342.htm

• Page 219: "A monk reading"
https://www.freepik.es/fotos-premium/libro-lectura-monje-tailand-ia_3615152.htm

• Page 220: " Wat Phra That Pha Kaew"
https://www.freepik.es/foto-gratis/estatua-cinco-buda_1155948.htm#-from_element=cross_selling___photo

• Page 224: "Full Length Friends Sitting Home"
https://www.freepik.es/fotos-premium/monje-ensenando-nino-monasterio_98722924.htm

• Page 230: "A Monk Teaching To a Student"
https://www.freepik.es/fotos-premium/monje-esta-ensenando-religion-ni-nos-interesados-miercoles-templo-ayutthaya_17959288.htm

• Page 234: "Sanscrit Heart Sutra"
(Prajñāpāramitā Hridaya Sūtra in siddham script)
https://commons.wikimedia.org/wiki/File:Prajnyaapaaramitaa_Hridaya_Pel.sogd.jpg#/media/

www.ingramcontent.com/pod-product-compliance
Lightning Source LLC
Chambersburg PA
CBHW060316050426
42449CB00011B/2507